For Clark Ellison -
a friend in the
faith .

Jim W Groffat

(Philippians 4:13)

Sure You Can

SURE
YOU
CAN

Jim N. Griffith

Broadman Press
Nashville, Tennessee

4282–63 (BRP)
4252–63 (trade)
ISBN: 0–8054–5263–x (trade)

Dewey Decimal Classification: 248.4
Subject heading: CHRISTIAN LIFE
Library of Congress Catalog Card Number: 77–91269
Printed in the United States of America

Dedicated to my wife, Mimi, who, during all of our years together, has joined hands and heart with me on the glorious highway of faith that leads to surety even in the midst of obscurity.

Preface

The old saying has it that *"can't* never did anything." But this is not exactly right. *Can't* has done plenty.

Down through the centuries *can't* has stifled enthusiasm, sabotaged dreams, impeded progress, and smothered happiness.

It has broken hearts, ruined lives, and retarded spiritual growth.

Can't, the Goliath of discouragement, has wounded countless victims and left them stranded on the battlefield of life.

But here, in the sling of these pages, are three smooth stones of affirmation which, if they find their mark like David's missile, can prove to be the killer of Giant Can't.

They are the words: Sure You Can.

—Jim N. Griffith

Acknowledgments

Gratitude is expressed to the members of my four congregations: Lakeside Baptist Church, North Myrtle Beach, South Carolina; First Baptist Church, Gray, Georgia; First Baptist Church, Saint Simons Island, Georgia, and Beech Haven Baptist Church, Athens, Georgia—all of whom allowed me to accompany them through sunshine and storm on a spiritual pilgrimage to the discovery that in all the needs of life God is sufficient.

And to my able secretary, Mrs. Brinda Stanley, who typed the final manuscript.

Unless otherwise noted, all Scripture quotations are from the King James Version of the Bible. Other biblical quotations are the author's interpretation.

Contents

1
Sure You Can

"But with God, all things are possible" (*Matt. 19:26*)

A man who came one day to my office at the church said he had heard my daily radio program and wanted to meet me.

The radio series, *The Brighter Side* seemed to have unusual appeal for this man and as I learned more about him I understood why.

He had waged a long-standing battle with alcohol and was, by any measurement, an old bottle-scarred veteran. There had been times in his life when the sun had gone under a cloud and darkness shrouded his every step. He had learned through the microscope of experience that if we are to find the brighter side of life, we have to look for it.

When he stood to leave, he asked if I would come and speak to a group of alcoholics—friends of his who gathered each week for prayer and inspiration and, hopefully, declaration of another week of sobriety.

The date was set and entered on my calendar. Two weeks later, as I was leaving home for this speaking engagement, my wife asked: "What are you going to say to those folks?"

Thinking a moment, I said, "I'm going to tell them they can!"

"That's what they need to hear," she said.

As I looked into their faces, lined by the past like a road map over rough terrain, I was even more convinced that they needed to be told, "You can. You can win out over this problem."

But as I drove home, following my message, I was reminded of the young and enthusiastic theological student who was once asked to speak at the Bowery Mission in New York City. Proud of his ability as an orator and basking in the warmth of his evangelistic zeal, he preached with great force and vitality and ended his sermon by reciting the poem *If* by Rudyard Kipling:

> If you can keep your head when all about you
> Are losing theirs and blaming it on you,
> If you can trust yourself when all men doubt you;
> But make allowances for their doubting too;
> If you can dream and not make dreams your master;
> If you can think and not make thoughts your aim;
> If you can meet with Triumph and Disaster
> And treat those two imposters just the same.[1]

So on he went until he brought the poem to a dramatic conclusion, and then a whiskey-soaked voice in the back of the hall spoke up and said, "Well, what if you can't?"[2]

One wonders if this startling question was greeted only by stunned silence.

Did faith answer and echo through the hall? Replying with the words needed by every despairing soul: "Sure you can!" Was there some Christian brother ready to seek out the man with a you-can suggestion that encouraged his heart and stiffened his backbone?

This is a delicate subject to discuss. The line between *I can't* and *I can* is often finely drawn. There are I can'ts that must be recognized, either permanently or temporarily.

Vince Lombardi, the late great football coach of the Green Bay Packers, was an unusual and determined man —almost to the point of fanaticism. But his philosophy of

"Winning isn't everything, it's the only thing" doesn't always hold up.

This concept, when carried to the extreme, can tear the heart out of those who feel that they simply cannot win.

However, the Christian faith, in its finest hours, not only shows us how to win but also it shows us how to lose and cope with the loss.

The painful truth is we do live under certain limitations, both physical and mental. There are differences in endowment, talent, and ability. But the question is: With what you have, do you accentuate the positive or the negative?

In one developmental seminar, one question is always asked of all those who seek the better life. The question is: Who first slapped you back into your dark little space? Or in other words, who pushed you into a corner? Who stepped on you? Who holds you back? Who hinders you?

Of course, despite all opinions to the contrary, the logical answer to all these questions is *you*. You are the culprit. You, by your attitudes, hinder yourself.

The defeatist attitude almost never wins. The victorious attitude almost never loses.

Carlyle Marney tells of the delightful five-year-old boy who comes by his house each evening for their daily "roughhouse and wrestling" appointment.

One day, the vigorous little chap had kung-fued Marney, had assaulted him—hip and thigh and teeth—until, in exasperation, the older battler rolled over two hundred pounds on the younger battler's forty pounds and pinned him to the floor—hoof, horn, and nostril.

But then, with eyes wide open, fist and teeth clinched as if in mortal combat, struggling against overpowering odds, the five-year-old warrior said, "Even when I'm on the bottom, I'm winning!"

Keeping this same determination as he grows to manhood should mean that this youngster will never be defeated—at least, not for long. He may be down—but not out.

Of course, there are I can'ts which must be accepted. But we must never succumb to an I can't. The word *succumb* means to lie down and sink under.

No negative thought should submerge us. We need not sink in the mire of discouragement because of an inability. It is possible to rise.

But what if you can't? That is the great *if* of life.

What if you can't handle yourself?

What if your problems are too much for you?

What if you can't conquer your temptation?

What if you can't get rid of that feeling of guilt?

What if you have a weakness of temperament or disposition that defeats you?

What if there is a situation that drags you down to the depths?

What if you have a habit that you detest and you can't master it? What if you have an ideal and you can't reach it?

How shall we deal with these I can'ts?

We can appeal to Christ who waits to help us.

Man's extremity is always God's opportunity.

Even a primitive, pagan man in the wilds of the jungle reaches out for the spirits to help him. If he believes that the spirit resides in a tree or a stone, you will find him trying to influence that tree or stone with a sacrificial offering. He expects a feat of magic. He believes in bad spirits and good. He will beg the bad spirits not to hinder the good spirits' desire to help.

It is instinctive and natural when one cannot handle a situation to ask the unseen powers for assistance.

So it is that the Christian believer calls on the higher

power, as found only in Jesus Christ, to assist in the face of difficult situations.

We appeal to Christ to help us because we realize that there are things we cannot do alone.

When a great old missionary to Africa went into the jungle for the last time, he cried out, just as he had on his first wilderness journey, "I cannot do it alone!" And again his prayer was answered as he went straight forward and entered the jungle. He did not go alone. Jesus was with him.

To reach the highest mountain peak, one must be tied securely to a guide. There are spiritual heights that can be climbed only with the assistance of another: the heavenly guide, Jesus Christ.

There are numerous things we cannot do until we pray, "Thy will be done" (Matt. 26:42). Jesus prayed in the garden of Gethsemane that the cup of suffering might pass from him. It was a bitter cup to drink. When he uttered the words, "Not my will, but thine, be done" (Luke 22:42), his victory was won.

Prayer is the appeal of the soul to God, but it is also a surrender of the will unto God. In appealing to God, we should make certain that the purpose or aim on our part is valid in the name of Christ. Jesus said, "Whatsoever ye shall ask in my name, that will I do, that the Father may be glorified in the Son" (John 14:13).

The first step then in dealing with an I can't is to appeal to God through Christ for help.

A second step is to accept responsibility for yourself, your sins, your shortcomings.

Do not run away from yourself. An observant young man had just returned from a visit to the town in which he had been born and reared. As always, there had been changes.

"The saddest thing about the community," he said, with a catch in his voice, "is that everyone seems to be trying to run away from himself."

The sin of his hometown is a widespread sin of our times. Literally millions of people are trying to run away from themselves. Sadly, they meet with no more success than the vain attempt to escape one's shadow under the rays of a bright sun.

A troubled young woman says, "If I could only get away from myself. It seems that at every turn I meet myself in some disgusting fashion."

Often the hardest thing to face is oneself. But we must face ourselves and accept the responsibility for our sins and shortcomings. There is no escape from self except escape on the higher level of surrender to the saving power of Jesus Christ.

To do this, we must be willing to accept the discipline of God. We have fooled ourselves into disliking even the word *discipline* and thereby deluded ourselves into flabbiness of character. The path of least resistance is a well-worn path that leads to misery and many of us are inclined to walk in it.

By the lack of discipline, even though we may ask God for help, we make ourselves impossible for God to reach with his helping hand.

A third point in accepting responsibility for oneself is to be patient and willing to advance slowly in quest of the good life.

Although this is the age of speed, the pull is often slow on the road to the good and useful Christian life. Climbing the Mount Everest of the soul is step by step. There is no shortcut to achievement—one must be patient. Overnight success is often over in a night.

A youth, who was admittedly guilty of some very serious drug abuses and other related offenses, came to the point of self-discovery and assumed responsibility for his sins and shortcomings. The first step he took on the road back was to set out in an entirely new direction that led to Jesus Christ and the Christian life.

At the end of the first week he reported to his pastor, "My week has been clean." The minister rejoiced with him as the young man shouted, "Oh the joy of being clean again for one whole week!"

Sometime later he said, "I now have five clean weeks to my credit." And so he held on, and by holding on to Christ, he patiently and slowly moved to the new life.

A final step in dealing with the negative I can't is to hold on to a belief in the miraculous.

Jesus Christ still walks among us. Look at the incident from the Gospel of John. Here was a crowd of sick people, blind, lame, and paralyzed.

Among them was a man who had been crippled for thirty-eight years.

Jesus saw him, spoke to him, and said, "Rise to your feet, take up your bed and walk" (John 5:8, author's translation). There was the miraculous event! The man stood to his feet and walked.

Have we seen any miraculous changes in the lives of the people of our day? Surely we have, if our eyes have been open.

I have seen a down-and-out derelict of a man who cried out, "I can't," win a victory through this miraculous changing power of Jesus Christ.

I have seen a hard, bitter, unlikable, unlovely woman change into a sweet and gentle person. There are many such transformations to be seen all about us. Our Lord is a worker of miracles. His ways are higher than our ways.

The old yardman, full of years and faith, said it well in

his daily prayer of affirmation, "O Lord, always help me to remember that there ain't nothing that you and me together can't handle."

What if we can't? What of it? Our Lord can. With God, all things are possible!

2

Your Life: A Mess or a Message?

Whoever has the Son has this life; whoever does not have the Son of God does not have life (1 John 5:12, author's translation).

Charles Dickens, in one of his writings, sounded as if he could have been looking over our shoulders and reading today's newspaper: "It was the best of times, it was the worst of times, it was the age of wisdom, it was the age of foolishness, . . . it was the season of Light, it was the season of Darkness, it was the spring of hope, it was the winter of despair."

Ours is an age of the paradox. We have more law and less order, more wealth and more poverty, more religion and less faith, more comfort and more fear. Grimm's Fairy Tales have been replaced by "grim and scary tales" of trouble at home and abroad.

Little boys, talking among themselves, now ask: "What are you going to be—if you grow up?" Manufacturers have even placed a new toy on the market which is designed to equip a child to live in today's world. It seems that no matter how you put it together, it comes out wrong.

The signs of our times reveal the unrest all about us. There is the heading over a bulletin board in the United States State Department: Today's Crisis. And with some, there is surrender to futility resulting in unconcern as expressed in a sign printed in large block letters by a university student: DUE TO LACK OF INTEREST, TOMORROW WILL BE CANCELED.

But I want to tell you of another sign which I saw outside the chapel of a school of nursing. It asked a question which we need to ask: Will your life be a mess or a message? It is your choice, your decision.

I believe our Lord would have asked the same question. Jesus declared: "Ye have heard that it was said by them of old time . . . but I say unto you" (Matt. 5:21–22). To use the saying of the day, Jesus told it like it was. Jesus says it like it is. Christ speaks to you today. Now. Where you are.

"You have heard it said of old, but I say unto you," Jesus said. He did not come to put his rubber stamp upon the past. He came with a whole new idea, and it captured the hearts and minds of his generation! Jesus caught the imagination of his disciples because he was not satisfied to put new wine into old wineskins.

Kierkegaard, the Danish theologian, said: "Every generation must face Jesus Christ anew." There are many things we must inherit but Christian experience is not one of them. Christian faith is something we must experience for ourselves. The Scripture makes this very plain: "He who has the Son has this life, He who does not have the Son of God does not have life" (1 John 5:12, author's translation). Christ must happen to you. Too often our Christianity is something which happens outside of us. We can stand off and watch it take place with little thought of personal transformation or involvement.

One day two small boys went into a dentist's office. One said to the dentist, "I want a tooth taken out and I don't want any gas, and I don't want it deadened because I'm in a hurry."

"Well," said the dentist, "I must say you are a brave little boy. Which tooth is it?" The boy turned to his smaller silent friend and said, "Show him your tooth, Albert."

This is true in the spiritual life. We are anxious to have something happen—to someone else. In one biblical incident: "A great multitude followed [Jesus]" (John 6:2). Why? That he might rid their lives of hatred, jealousy, selfishness? That he might lead them into a life of loving service to others? No! They followed Jesus, the Scripture tells us, "Because they saw his miracles which he did on them that were diseased" (John 6:2). Few had any thoughts of personal repentance, surrender, or spiritual rebirth. They wanted to see Jesus do something to somebody else. And much of today's following of Christ has the same shallow motivation. We want to see God change the world but are not eager for Christ to change us. But each and every generation must face Jesus Christ anew.

As one Christian said: "It does something to you when you personally know and have a Christ who lives among you and looks you in the eye." And if your life is to be a radiant Christian message, there are at least three things that the Christianity of today must do in you and for you.

First, your Christianity must be intellectually honest.

One Sunday at church a woman came up and shook hands with her minister and said: "You just don't know what a help your sermons have been to my husband since he lost his mind."

Frequently, it is assumed that a religious experience doesn't involve any mental exercise. Nothing could be further from the truth. It is interesting to note that Jesus did not quote the law of Moses just as it was when he cited the commandment: "Thou shalt love the Lord thy God with all thy heart, with all thy soul, and with all thy mind, and with all thy strength" (Mark 12:30). The sixth chapter of Deuteronomy speaks of loving God with your heart, soul, and strength. The writer leaves the mind out. Jesus put it in!

Often a minister hears the complaint that we don't have enough emotion in our religion. And to a certain point, I agree! But for every person who has left the heart out of his religion, I know of many more who have left the head out.

From the able pen of Henry Van Dyke hear these words:

> Four things a man must learn to do if he would
> write his record true;
> To think, without confusion, clearly;
> To love his fellowmen sincerely;
> To act from honest motives purely;
> To trust in God and Heaven securely.

Perhaps the hardest is the first—to think without confusion, clearly. We can no longer steal answers to our questions from our ancestors. We must think out for ourselves today's answers for today's questions.

If you are a doubter by nature, then I suggest that you perform a bit of surgery on your doubts. Go ahead and cut away. Bleed a little bit. Surgery is always painful. But the result, if you are honest with yourself, is that in the end you will have a healthy faith, one robust enough to stand up to the questions that life keeps throwing at you. But, after you have performed this surgery, be sure that the faith you have is your own. Hearts may be transplanted by today's doctors, but Christian experience must be your own.

When Oliver Cromwell sat for a portrait, the artist left off the big warts on his face. When the work was finished, Cromwell said to the artist: "It's quite good, but it isn't honest. You left off my warts. Paint me again, warts and all; then it will look like the real Cromwell." And so it must be. No illusion, no sham, no pretense—just trying to see the truth, warts and all. It all begins, you see, with intellectual honesty! To love God, we must love him with our minds as well as our hearts.

Then, too, if your life is to be a message, your Christianity must be morally demanding.

A great deal has been written and said about the present generation being the most undisciplined generation in history. This may be true. But in talking to young people, I get the impression that most are looking for some moral disciplines and yardsticks by which to measure their conduct.

I am not suggesting a return to the old puritanical religion built on a system of "Thou shalt nots." I am saying that we need to rediscover that connecting link between what we believe and what we do!

When a minister moves among people, he runs into almost as many ideas of religion as there are people. The one with which he has least patience is that which professes great faith in God and yet complains all the time in fault-finding sadness about life's misfortunes.

I read of a minister who endured such an attitude in one of his members as long as he could. When testimony time came in the service, this woman would always stand and moan: "O Lord, if I had the wings of a dove I'd fly away from this land of sin and tears and at last be at rest."

One night when she had again made such a request, the preacher spoke out before he thought: "Stick another feather in her, Lord, and let her go!"

The fact is, Christianity does not kill joy; it adds to joy. If you have the right kind of faith, it ought to add to your total amount of happiness, not contribute to your misery. Christianity is not a restraint but an inspiration—not a subtraction but an addition.

What we need today is a new discipline—a disciplined life—not because we are under law but because we are under grace. The truth has made us free, free to serve God because we love him. If you love God, you will obey his commandments. But let we warn you that this is impossible unless Jesus Christ lives in you. I do not believe that anyone can be a dynamic follower of Christ unless his life has been surrendered to Christ. "He who has the Son has this life; he who does not have the Son of God has not life" (1 John 5:12, author's translation).

Our Christianity must be morally demanding. Our moral signals must be well defined and read loud and clear. We must have a faith that has some moral fiber in it, a commitment that makes a difference in the kind of person we are. A faith on which a sound life can be built.

I came across such a faith in a young university couple who joined my church. The young man, former all-American basketball player, moved with his lovely wife to our university city to continue his studies for a doctoral degree. In the process of moving, the young wife had fallen and broken her leg. But the doctor had put it in a cast and she went merrily clanking along. They moved into their apartment on Saturday, left the packing boxes stacked to the ceiling, and came to church Sunday morning, broken leg and all.

I visited the next day with this bright, handsome couple. And the young man said, "Pastor, we are joining your church. And I can promise you this: We will be there for every service; God comes first with us." For these radiant Christians, life is a message and not a mess. But you cannot have this kind of faith and dedication unless you are among those who have life because they first of all have the Son of God.

I recall when they came forward to transfer their membership to our church. This young man stuck out his hand, and said, "Pastor, give me the hardest job you've got."

This young man and woman, wholly committed to Christ, wanted a challenge. And so it is that if we are to meet the desperate needs of our day, we must embrace the kind of Christian faith that seeks and accepts the challenge.

There is a story about a young man who was proposing to his girl. Said he, "I am not wealthy and I don't have a yacht and convertible like Jerome Green, but my darling, I love you." The girl thought for a moment and then replied: "And I love you, too; but tell me a little more about Jerome." Here is the common failing of many. They know the way and they know the right person, but they cannot refrain from asking to learn a little more about something that promises an easier time and richer reward.

One of the greatest virtues and one of the most difficult to practice is commitment. Blessed is that person who has so committed himself that he no longer is tempted to turn aside for some conflicting interest. This is the essential secret of the Christian life. Once having chosen the right way, nothing ever seems to turn the fully dedicated person aside from his Christian goal. He has been challenged, and he accepts the challenge and commits himself to the task. Here is where one hears criticism of youth today. Some have not accepted the challenge or committed themselves to great things.

One episode of "Peanuts," the popular comic strip, had two girls talking about Charlie Brown. One said, "Charlie Brown is pretty clever sometimes. Three big boys from the second grade chased him today and he ran and ran, but they kept getting closer and closer. Suddenly, Charlie Brown stopped and organized a discussion group."

That seems to be about the only answer some people can offer to the problems of our day: Organize a discussion group. But discussion groups won't ever take the place of people who accept the challenge before them and give their lives to Christ.

Do you remember Charles Dickens' story *A Tale of Two Cities?* There is a moving scene in which Sydney Carton is giving his life for his friend. A young girl has watched this man's courage and hopes that his strength will give her strength, "If I may ride with you," she asks, "will you let me hold your hand? I am not afraid, but I am a little weak and it will give me more courage." When the cart reaches the place of execution, the girl looks up into the man's face and says, "I think you were sent me by heaven."

The right man—Jesus Christ our Master—is on our side. Sent to us from heaven, he says: "Give me your hand. Come walk with me today and into tomorrow." The darkness you fear is but the shadow of God's brightness. For "he who has the Son of God has life" (1 John 5:12).

3
You Will Find Strength Through Weakness

Which of you by [being anxious] can add one cubit to his stature? (Matt. 6:27).

The crowd must have smiled at these words of Jesus. "Which of you," Jesus said, "by [being anxious] can add one cubit to his stature?" (Matt. 6:27).

This question asked by our Lord spotlights a situation which is so true to life. Picture the children at home measuring themselves on the wall to find out how much they have grown. Perhaps you remember how you, as a little girl or boy, longed to grow tall. I can remember quite well when I was in my last year in grammar school. I was suffering through that stage in life when all of the girls, who always seem to grow faster than boys, were at least two heads taller than I.

It was a trying time for me. I had to look up to every girl in my class.

I couldn't see eye to eye with any of the girls.

I ate my spinach, as Popeye suggested, but it was no use. I did not seem to grow taller. I was anxious enough, but, as Jesus declares in the text, my anxiety did not add one inch to my height.

And yet, Jesus was not talking to children or even about children, but to grown-up people who should know better.

How foolish people are, Jesus was saying, how foolish they are to spoil their lives in their anxiety to grow bigger, to become more influential and wealthier than their neighbors.

How foolish to see them posing, pretending, and impressing nobody, deceiving nobody except themselves.

Of course, when Jesus said, "Be not anxious," he didn't mean that we should not plan and work for a better future; for without direction and purpose, life becomes a futile existence.

Certainly we must set our standards high and resolve to make our dreams come true. But we must at the same time do this: We must set out in life with a real desire to give our heart to the world so that our daily work may be more than just the means of earning a living and with this unselfish attitude make a distinct contribution to the common good of all.

Another very important thing to remember is that when we are planning and dreaming, it is wise to remember our human limitations.

There are certain limitations in life: We don't all grow tall; we don't all wear the same size shoe; we don't all have big muscles.

And there are certain intellectual, as well as physical limitations: We can't all translate Latin prose or work out difficult mathematical problems. There is a variety in human nature. We are all different in gifts, in nature, in temperament, and in ability.

But do not misunderstand me. I am not advocating a pious resignation to our inabilities. God forbid that I should do that. What I am saying is this: There is strength, great strength, to be had in the realistic acceptance of ourselves as we are so that by the strength and love of God we may grow and develop into the fullness of what God would have us to be as he gives us the skill for every task to which he directs us.

The experience of Mrs. Rosalynn Carter, wife of the President of the United States, supports this truth.

She said: "I never made speeches until Jimmy was governor. I didn't think I could do anything like that." [1]

Then, one day there was a dramatic change from weakness to strength—from nervousness on the platform to calm assurance.

"Somebody," she declared, "sent me this little tract, entitled, 'Lovingly in the hands of the Father,' and it simply stated that if you put yourself at all times completely in the hands of the Lord, He will take care of you all the time and you can go ahead and do anything you have to do." [2]

The result was that she made the happy discovery that she could get up in front of large crowds, think to herself, I'm in the loving hands of the Father, and then look them straight in the eyes and talk to them and not be afraid that she was doing it wrong or worry about what they might think of her.

Conscientious wife that she is, Rosalynn once told her husband of her fear that she might say something that would hurt him. The man who was to become President looked at his wife and asked: "Before you speak, don't you pray, 'God help me, God help me?' "

"Why," she replied, "yes, I do."

"Then," said Carter, "that's all that's necessary. You just ask the Lord to help you do the best you can and you will do all right." [3]

Humility is the key which unlocks the gate and lets man set foot on the path of faith where the journey can be made from weakness to strength.

All persons, though beset with human frailties, are on their way to being something when they realize that in themselves they are nothing but that God is everything, and God can make something out of nothing.

There is power, wonder-working power, available to

those of us who will come to an acceptance of ourselves as we are. That is not easy to do. It demands fearless honesty and absolute sincerity.

But the point at which I start on the road to improvement is when I realize my limitations and see myself exactly as I am and then decide to do something about it through the uplifting strength of Jesus Christ.

There is in our day and time too much self-pity, too much feeling sorry for ourselves. We look at others and moan: "They seem to be far more fortunate than we are, they seem to do so much and we are in a rut."

Doesn't everyone have to live life within certain limitations? Aren't we all in a rut, so to speak? The good news is that this rut does not have to become a grave.

A young preacher, not yet dry behind his ministerial ears, went to see an old minister friend of his, a man who had many years of valuable experience in the ministry.

The old man welcomed the young preacher into his study and motioned for him to have a seat. "Now, tell me how everything is going in your church," the old preacher said.

"Well," said the young man in a discouraged tone of voice, "we are doing about as well as could be expected under the circumstances."

"Under the circumstances," the old man exclaimed, "what are you doing *under* the circumstances? Get on *top* of the circumstances!"

Jesus is our supreme example of true greatness. He never sought power or position. He sought to do the job at hand faithfully and well. What did he seek to do? To guide the perplexed and strengthen the weak. To raise the fallen and rescue the perishing. His mission is still the same today, and his strength is available to all.

Of all men, the apostle Paul was most conscious of his

weakness and limitations, yet he could boast, "I can do all things through Christ which strengtheneth me" (Phil. 4:13).

There was strength to come out of his weakness.

The roll call of God's heroes, in the epistle to the Hebrews is prefaced by the words: Those who "out of weakness were made strong" (Heb. 11:34).

Hudson Taylor, the founder of a mission in China, once said: "When God sought me out and called me to do His work in China, He must have said: 'This man is weak enough, he will do.'"

We know what this missionary meant. He was saying that the secret of spiritual power is to be aware of our weakness and cast ourselves upon God. For it is just at the moment that we confess our failings that we are most fully conscious of God's willingness to give us a lift at the point of life's lowest ebb.

We can see a mother nursing her sick child with loving care, day and night watching by the bedside.

"How can she stand the strain?" we may ask. She would answer simply: "I have been given strength—strength not my own—strength above and beyond myself."

Consider the businessman who, besides the heavy responsibility of his work, is worried about his wife's failing health. And yet, he never complains. Indeed, he has a cheerful word for everyone.

Many know and would testify from personal experiences that when the need is greatest, they are not left alone.

It is in the ordinary demands of everyday life that we are given the opportunity to prove to ourselves just where we are, in our particular situation with all its hardships, to prove that God's grace is sufficient for all our daily needs.

There is an old story of an artist whose hand was losing its skill and whose eyes were becoming dim. Every night when he retired he was more and more depressed with his work. But while he was asleep his son would creep downstairs and retouch his father's painting. In the morning the old man would look at the canvas and say, "Well, it is not as bad as I thought."

In just the same way our lives are renewed and retouched by the living presence of Christ. And we, in our weakness, can be strengthened by the skill of the Son of God as we look at the picture of life and say: "It is not as bad as I thought."

4
Why Are You Afraid?

He said unto them, "Why are you afraid? Have you no faith?" (Mark 4:40, RSV).

The late President Franklin Delano Roosevelt once addressed Congress and an anxious nation with these reassuring words: "We have nothing to fear but fear itself." The fear that President Roosevelt sought to assuage in 1933 was the panic of a depression time. Many were paralyzed by their fears.[1]

To a worried nation these words were comforting, encouraging, and reassuring. We needed those words then, and we need them again today.

Almost everyone in our day is afraid of something. Two friends had stopped on the street to chat.

Said one: "So, you've been going to a psychiatrist? Has he helped you?"

"Sure," replied the friend. "I used to be deathly afraid to answer the telephone. Now, I answer it whether it rings or not." [2]

The validity of his cure is open to debate. But it is certain that life for this man, just as with many others, is filled with fear.

Some people are afraid of life with its terrific responsibilities. Others have abnormal fears of death and live under constant dread that life will be snuffed out at any moment. Some are afraid of high places, while others fear a closed room and being caught in small places.

There are those who fear elevators and some who fear steps. Others are afraid to ride and some are afraid to walk.

Countless fears prevail in the lives of many persons. Their boats always seem to be rocking on the stormy sea of life. This brings to mind an incident in the life of Jesus (Mark 4:35–41).

At the close of a strenuous day of teaching, Jesus turned to his disciples and said: "Let us go over to the other side, away from the crowd." He was tired. Hence, in the twilight of that summer evening, the disciples lifted anchor, Jesus got into the stern of the boat, and before long the cool evening breezes, coming across the Sea of Galilee, relaxed him so that he fell asleep.

When they were halfway across the body of water, a quick storm appeared. The heat of the day had cooked it up, and it suddenly descended upon them. The Sea of Galilee is not too deep, and, like all shallow bodies of water, the wind can whip it into a frenzy. The disciples were fishermen. They were boating enthusiasts. But before long these seasoned fishermen were scared stiff. They were in a panic.

The story tells us that their boat was heaving so that it was spilling water. And there was their Master, their Teacher, sound asleep. Finally, they could stand it no longer. They were terrified. They thought they were going to sink, and, in desperation, they woke him and said: "Master, don't you care whether we perish?"

Jesus stood up, looked at his disciples, then at the waves and faced into the wind saying: "Peace! Be still!"

In a short while the wind ceased and the waves calmed and then he asked the disciples two questions. The first one: "Why are you afraid?" And the second one, still more penetrating and yet reassuring, "Have you no faith?"

This story of Jesus and his disciples strikes me as being as up-to-date as today's newspaper. This incident speaks to us. For the fact is, the disciples' boat is not the only one that has rocked on the sea of life. Most of us who have grown to maturity know that on more than one occasion our own boat of life has come very close to capsizing—buffeted about—until we have become inwardly terrified.

Although we may stand with voices lifted high and sing, "Cast thy burden on the Lord," our hearts still reflect a worried mind. And if we are left to our own resources, we are apt to get into a state of terror, thinking that all is lost. This is exactly the position the disciples were in, yet they were skilled fishermen, most of them. They had been out in boats often enough, but this time it seemed too much for them. They needed help beyond themselves. So they called out to Jesus who alone could save them.

How fortunate we are, when the storms of life assail us and our boats of life seem about to capsize, that we, too, can call out to the Son of the living God to help us. He never fails us.

Years ago, Dr. Louie D. Newton, well-known Atlanta minister and writer, boarded a plane and sat down beside a young mother and her five-month-old daughter. As the plane climbed high above the clouds they began to talk. The mother and child were on their way to Los Angeles.

"It is a difficult trip for us to take," she said. "We are going to California to meet my husband's body . . . he was killed in the war. We just had to come and meet him. He has never seen his daughter, but I wanted her to go along with me. Maybe someway, somehow, he knows that we are meeting his body."

Just then the plane, preparing to land, started down through the clouds, and there in the folds of the clouds was a beautiful rainbow! The woman, tears shining in her eyes, said softly, "I never thought I would see another rainbow. But God's promises never fail. His light always shines through the clouds."

It is interesting to note what Jesus says to us when we

call out in our fears and anxiety for help. As with the disciples on the stormy Sea of Galilee, he asks you in your panic, in your anxiety, and in your fear: "Why are you afraid?" And you have to answer that question. You must have the courage to take out some of the major fears of your life, the ones that really rock your boat, and then ask of yourself Christ's question: "Why am I afraid?"

Could it be that for most of us we have temporarily lost our anchor? We have cut ourselves adrift and when the boat rocks and we have no anchor and we are drifting and we are out of communication with Christ who can save us, panic and fear and anxiety swallow us.

You recall the old familiar hymn:

> Will your anchor hold in the storms of life,
> When the clouds unfold their wings of strife,
> When the strong tides lift, and the cables strain,
> Will your anchor drift, or firm remain?

Then comes back the resounding chorus of assurance:

> We have an anchor that keeps the soul
> Steadfast and sure while the billows roll,
> Fastened to the Rock which cannot move,
> Grounded firm and deep in the Saviour's love.

Yes, Jesus asks: "Why are you afraid?" And somewhat shamefully we have to admit that, in our panic and tension in these modern days, we have forgotten him who is always with us.

Then Jesus presses us still further with a second question: "Have you no faith?" Surely with Christ present in the boat the disciples should have had faith that all would be well. They might get awfully wet, of course, but it just could not end in their destruction.

This comforting truth was also discovered by a wealthy

New York businessman who lost everything he had in the stock market crash of 1929. At first, he went to pieces. Some friends who had been fortunate enough to salvage some scattered funds and holdings offered to back him with a loan, but he was quick to say, "No, I am through, I am all washed up!" He told them that in his present state of physical and mental collapse, he was not to be trusted with other people's money.

His loving wife had a thousand dollars in her savings account and with that she took him to a quiet little place in Florida near a beautiful lake. She hoped and prayed that he would find himself again, recover his physical and mental health, and be a well man.

Her husband would sit on the bank of the lake by the hour staring into the placid water. He could not sleep and he could not eat. He kept repeating to himself that he was a failure. His basic security which had been money was gone.

One day in the backwoods section around the lake, the man was strolling back to his cottage when he saw a big bully of a boy beating a smaller lad. And in trying to stop the tussle, he pushed the larger boy into a tree so hard it scratched his face. The boy, huge for his age, flew into a temper tantrum, shook his fist in the air, and vowed that his papa would settle the man's hash in short order.

That evening the young ruffian returned to the man's cottage to say that his papa would be over bright and early the next morning and that he had better get out of town if he did not want to get shot.

Then a friendly neighbor dropped by to say that the old backwoodsman, the father of the boy, was half drunk and had been down at the village telling his cronies that no "city slicker" could draw blood on his boy without paying with his life.

The fearful and dejected man lay awake all night. Here was something that had to be faced. Running away would only deepen his mental torment. He arose quietly at 4 A.M. and started for the backwoodsman's home. He would walk straight into the jaws of death and die facing his enemy. Strangely enough, as he walked along the road on his grim errand he did not feel alone. He was no longer afraid. God suddenly seemed friendly and close to him and real to him. The sunrise looked beautiful as the big golden ball appeared over the Everglades.

He knocked on the old man's door and was confronted by the angry father himself, rifle in hand. But even as he looked at this frightening picture, he was smiling and unafraid as he said: "I'm not armed. You can go ahead and shoot me at your pleasure, but before you do, I'd like to have a little talk with you."

The old fellow put down his gun. "I can't shoot an unarmed man on my doorstep," he said. "Especially not a brave man like you."

They talked and made their peace. After shaking hands with the father of the boy, the man started back to his cottage near the lake.

When he arrived at the little cottage, his wife was waiting for him with tears in her eyes and arms outstretched. "I heard you when you left," she said, "and I also knew that you had to go. So I lay very still and prayed. After a short time a great peace came over me, and I knew you had found yourself again." And sure enough he had.

This man had conquered fear by doing two things. He accepted the situation as it was and went out to face it. He resolved never to run away from trouble again, but to confront it with faith in God and in himself. In so doing, God's miraculous power took possession of his fearful heart and the trouble evaporated into thin air.

That is the formula for overcoming any fear: face it. Move toward the thing you fear. And then turn the stream of your thoughts away from yourself toward God in the confidence that the strength of God is your strength. The result will be victory.

Look again at the words of Jesus: "Why are you afraid? Have you no faith?"

He was saying if you had faith, you would not be afraid. He stood in the midst of his disciples who trembled with fear at the windstorm. Their boat had been pounded by the waves, water had splashed into the boat, but Jesus slept on in peace until they, fearing for their lives, could stand it no longer. They aroused him from his sleep. "How can you sleep when we may perish in this boat?" But Jesus, in questioning them, diagnosed their trouble: You are afraid because you have no faith. They were thinking of themselves, not the power of God, not God's strength; they were thinking of their weakness.

Fear paralyzes, faith empowers; fear disheartens, faith encourages; fear sickens, faith heals. Fear destroys, faith saves.

At this point, someone may be thinking—some fear-dazed person may be thinking: "I agree with all this, but I still keep on with the old treadmill of fear, getting precisely nowhere with my fine resolves to break loose."

Well, the way to begin the hopeful faith-way-of-life is to begin and begin now. As Andrew Jackson once said, "The way to resume is to resume." Thinking about this vital matter of faith is not enough. We must step boldly forth and start acting as though God does care and does empower us, as he most certainly does.

A young preacher in his college days went one Sunday to conduct services in a small village church. He stayed in a quaint old house occupied by the widow of a former minister. When he retired, he saw that he had been given her bedroom and in the morning when he pulled up the blinds, he saw that into the glass of the windowpane had been cut the words: "This is the day. . . ." (Ps. 118:24).

He asked the old lady about it at breakfast. She explained that she had had a lot of trouble in her time and was always afraid of what was going to happen on the morrow. Each morning as she woke she felt that she had the weight of the world upon her. One day as she was reading her Bible she came across the words: "This is the day. . . ." It occurred to her that it means any day, every day, this day. "Why," she asked, "should I be afraid of the days? God makes them. God makes all of them."

So she scratched the words, as well as she could, on the windowpane so that every time she drew her blinds in the morning she was confronted with the reminder, "This is the day. . . ." Realizing that the Lord had made the day, she was no longer afraid.

The world is full of people who wake up in the morning, dreading what the day may bring, or at least not looking forward to it. But it would make all the difference in the world if we could greet each day as a gift from God and say, "This is the day which the Lord hath made; we will rejoice and be glad in it."

God divides life into days. Any man can fight the battles of just one day. It is when we add the burdens of yesterday and our fears for tomorrow that we are liable to break down. In reality, there are no such things as good days and bad days. They are all God's days. The triumphant, victorious attitude is to make the most of today, free from anxiety about the future, because the God who cares for the smallest sparrow is quite capable of looking after our needs.

A preacher friend of mine before entering the ministry

ran two grocery stores and one wholesale grocery distributing firm. Ironically enough, there came a time, when he, with his family, was struggling through seminary when there was nothing to eat in his house. Late one Saturday afternoon his wife came to him with the sad news that the pantry was bare and there was no money left for the purchase of more groceries.

With a worried glance toward his three small children, the young preacher tried to comfort his wife with the words: "Never mind—a way will be provided." He left to make a visit and on the way he talked to the Lord. Earnestly, he said, "Lord, the Bible teaches that you know what we have need of even before we ask—so please, Lord, work out this difficulty. I place my trust in you."

Returning home, his wife met him at the door with a smile on her face. "There is a couple here to be married," she said. "They said you talked to them sometime ago."

As the young preacher walked in, the groom explained that they had to go right by the home of a number of ministers to get to him but for some reason they felt they should come to him. The preacher looked at his wife. She looked at him. They understood why the couple had been drawn to their house although it was several miles out of the way.

The ceremony was performed and the groom placed a generous wedding fee in the hand of the young minister. The grocery money had been provided. God will supply the needs of each day for he knows what things we have need of, even before we ask him.

Remembering this comforting word will do much to remove fear and insecurity from troubled lives. Never forget that this is God's world. He made it. He is our Father and he is all sufficient and all-good. These things being true, along with the assurance that even a sparrow cannot fall without his knowledge, we can live as children dwelling in the presence of a loving Father. "For God is our refuge and strength, a very present help in time of trouble. Therefore will not we fear, though the earth be removed, and though the mountains be carried into the midst of the sea" (Ps. 46:1-2).

If this is God's world, as we believe it to be, then God is not going to permit it to be scuttled, not even with several thousand hydrogen bomb blasts. The fears that literally tear us apart and bounce us around as tiny corks on the heavy sea of life until we are almost ready to give up— are they not mastering us because we have lost our faith, even momentarily?

The most important thing in dealing with fear is to stand up, face it, and defy it with faith in the power of Almighty God. In this way, you can overcome fear then and there.

Someone once asked a cowboy, a veteran rancher, what was the most important thing he had learned in all of his experiences. After a few moments of silence, he replied: "The Herefords taught me one of life's most important lessons. We were breeding cattle for a living, but the severe winter storms took an awful toll. Again and again after a bad winter storm we would find most of them piled up against the fences dead. They would turn their backs to the icy blasts of wind and slowly go drifting downwind about twenty miles until the fence stopped them. There they piled up and died."

"But," added the rancher, "the Herefords were different. They headed straight into the wind and slowly worked up the other way until they came to our upper boundary fence where they would continue to stand facing into the storm. We always found them alive and well. That is the greatest lesson I ever learned on these Western prairies."

And that is a supreme lesson for the victorious Christian life. Jesus stood up in the boat, with the high winds blowing all about him, and the waves dashing over the small craft. He faced the storm and said, "Peace! Be still!"

But it should be noted that to the disciples, as much as to the winds and waves, he said, "Peace, be still." It was the same assurance he gave them in the last hours of his ministry, while in the upper room, facing his own greatest crisis and storm, when he said to them: "Let not your heart be troubled. . . . My peace I give unto you" (John 14:1,27).

The boat of Jesus became calm and steady because he knew that although the way was difficult before him, though he could not run away or escape what lay ahead, all would be well and that, ultimately, there would be victory even over death itself.

Jesus gives to us peace of mind and soul as he calms the stormy waves and winds of anxiety. And, best of all, in time of need, whenever we call on him for help, he is there to confront us with his own reassuring presence.

And under his steadying hand, our boat stops rocking. He leads us beside the still waters and restores our souls.

It can be true in every life. Some years ago, a young child was given the responsibility of putting the empty milk bottles out on the front porch after the evening meal. One night he went to the door but came back with the bottles still in his arms.

Going to his father, he said, "It is too dark to go out there tonight without a father." When his father went out with him, he did not fear the dark. His father's presence gave him courage. And so it is with our heavenly Father.

It may be too frightening to go out into the darkness of the night of life without our loving heavenly Father. But he waits to accompany us.

Have you faced a problem that is too big for you to handle? Has some fear taken hold of you?

Then call on the Lord now while he is near. He is right in the boat with you.

It is true that Jesus will ask, "Why are you afraid? Have you no faith?"

But he will also say to you, "Peace! be still!"

And you will win the victory over fear. "For God has not given us a spirit of cowardice, but a spirit of power and of love and of self-control" [3] (2 Tim. 1:7).

5
You and Faith: Life's Great Essential

By faith the people crossed the Red Sea as if on dry land; but the Egyptians, when they attempted to do the same, were drowned (Heb. 11:29, RSV).

Faith is more than a word. It is a way of life.

The great resources of power in faith are almost beyond our imagination. God is life. His power touches all of life and we, by faith, can possess that power.

In Psalm 18 there is this passage: "And by my God I have leaped over a wall" (v. 29).

On innumerable occasions this has been true. Faith in God has enabled many persons to leap over the highest wall of difficulty, trouble, and distress.

Faith leaps walls and moves mountains. Faith specializes in the impossible.

Cowardice and faintheartedness says no, turn back. Faith says, yes—go on—move forward.

In an exciting incident recorded in the book of Hebrews, we have two ancient groups of people seeking to cross the barrier of the Red Sea. The Israelites made a successful crossing, but the Egyptians were swallowed up by the sea.

To one, the sea became a thoroughfare. To the other, it became a blind alley. One group sang the song of triumph, the other went down in defeat.

Why? Well, obviously, it was not because the Israelites were better equipped. On the contrary, they were a throng of newly liberated slaves while the Egyptians were supplied with horsemen, chariots, and other equipment for the venture. The reason that one group made a successful crossing and the other failed was because of an inward possession which the writer in Hebrews declares to be faith.

The Israelites possessed the one supreme essential in life: faith in God. And that is the supreme need for all people in the inevitable crossings of life.

Faith can take the sad song of life and make it a song of joy.

Faith can take the bleak picture of life, repaint it, and make it bright and beautiful.

What is faith? Faith is trusting God, yielding to God, and relying on God.

It is well to note the quality of faith shown in the lives of the ancient Israelites. For one thing, as in all true faith, it was a faith that inspired them. Having faith in God and his destiny for them, they followed Moses in seeking a better life. Faith in God can cause man to strive for higher levels of life.

The Egyptians were seeking to recover their lost property, but the Israelites were on the way to a Promised Land. Faith gives to life a goal and purpose. It is a journey to a Promised Land.

Furthermore, the faith of the Israelites was a conquering faith. Moses was not blind to the barrier, the sea before him and the children of Israel, but this man of God saw beyond his difficulty the power of God available through faith. And in the strength of that power, Moses and the multitude passed through the sea in safety while the Egyptians were drowned.

News reports carried the account of a thirteen-year-old second-class Boy Scout who was lost for seven days in the High Sierras. Remembering the woodsman's rule that water runs downhill and that following streams leads to safety, he plodded through brushy canyons, and at last came out, safe and sound.

His faith in following the stream to safety ought to suggest something to all who are lost in the far deeper woods of life. The one sure way to safety is through a conquering faith.

The Bible clearly teaches that if we have faith nothing is impossible for us. We can be like the bumblebee. According to recognized aerotechnical tests, the bumblebee cannot fly because of the shape and weight of his body in relation to the total wing area. However, the bumblebee doesn't know this, so he goes ahead and flies anyway.

Jesus said, "If you have faith as a grain of mustard seed, you can move mountains" (Matt. 17:20).

How then may we possess life's great essential? How may we deepen and enrich our faith in God? Here are a couple of simple suggestions: First, if we would deepen our faith, we must make much of the Bible. It is God's Book and in it we meet and know him. And through this increased knowledge of God there comes a greater faith.

We must also make much of the great privilege of prayer. It is through prayer and meditation, as in no other way, that God can impart strength to our lives. It is through prayer that we get on familiar terms with God.

Postal clerks in a Midwest city were at a loss one day as to what to do with a letter received in their office. They decided, after much deliberation, that it should go to the postmaster who was as perplexed as they.

The letter was addressed: "To the Lord, in care of Heaven."

It read: "Dear Lord: Please make my mommy well again."

The childish scrawl was signed: "Bobby."

This much is certain. No message sent to God in such wonderful childlike faith will ever find its way to the dead letter office, for God is nearer than the nearest post office.

And the Scripture says: "All things whatsoever ye shall ask in prayer, believing, ye shall receive" (Matt. 21:22).

Prayer is intimate conversation with God in which we open our hearts to him. We can talk to God as with a friend and in such hours we really come to know Christ. Communing with him, we are uplifted and given the faith to pass through the seas of difficulty.

To deepen and enrich our faith, we must look to Jesus. He is our reason for believing. He is the object of our faith. We must look past the prophets of gloom and look to Christ.

After all, the prophets of gloom are present in every age. In 1695, Thomas Beverly, a rector in the Church of England, wrote a book predicting that the world would end in 1697. He wrote a second book in 1698 complaining that the world had ended in 1697, but nobody had noticed.

Many face life with a similar attitude. The material, scientific and technical accomplishments of twentieth century man almost defy description. And yet, fear, mistrust, misery, and despair still abound. Pessimism is the order of the day.

There was a man and his wife, both well over ninety years old, whose seventy-year-old son had died. Returning from the funeral service, the old man said to his wife: "I told you we would never raise that boy."

Pessimism is everywhere. A friend said: "You know, if I found a four-leaf clover, I would get a slipped disc trying to pick it up."

In our panic-stricken day too many people belong to Pessimist International.

A well-known children's story, originally appearing in the first grade reader, reminds us that the lives of many burdened, sidetracked persons are similar to the experience of the heavily loaded, little train that wanted to get to the other side of the mountain.

Several larger engines passed on nearby tracks but refused to offer assistance. And then, when all seemed to be lost for the despairing train, there came puffing along Kind Little Blue Engine who was asked to assist the stranded train. As she hitched herself to the stalled train, and began the long, hard pull, she said, "I think I can. I think I can. I think I can."

Continuing to climb until she reached the top of the mountain, Little Blue Engine said, "I thought I could, I thought I could, I thought I could!" [1]

So it is with the power of faith. When we believe we can, we can—especially if our faith is in the living Lord of whom you may say: "I am enabled to do all things through Christ who is my strength" (see Phil. 4:13).

Faith not only removes mountains but also takes us over and around the mountains of life that would hamper and obstruct us.

And as one looks back at the mountain over which he has passed and offers a prayer of thanksgiving for the victorious journey, he sings a song of praise: "With the Lord's help, I knew I could!"

Of course, it goes without saying that none of us knows all the answers to the perplexities of our day.

It is like the woman who was being prepared for surgery. Her doctor told her they would have to give her gas to put her to sleep during the operation.

"Oh, doctor, will I know everything when I come out from under the gas?" she asked.

The doctor replied, "That's asking an awful lot of the gas!"

But we do know this: Looking through the window of

desperate need, one can see that having unfeigned faith in Jesus Christ is true knowledge and wisdom. We cannot expect to be equal to the needs of our day if we remain locked into our old defeatist mental attitudes.

Bishop Robert Goodrich said that he enjoyed going to the circus and before the performance began under the big tent, he liked to walk around and look at all the animals.

One time, to his surprise, he noticed that the chain was on the ground and the elephant was unchained.

Calling out to the attendant, he asked: "Did you know that your elephant is unchained?"

The trainer smiled and said, "Oh, we never chain him. We chained him at first, but now he just thinks he is chained."

The sad truth is that the elephant is like so many people. They do not move because they think they are chained. They are held back by past hindrances, frustrations, and disappointments.

But, like the elephant, they could walk away from the imaginary chains that bind them if they were willing to move forward in faith.

We must not be restrained by old defeatist, pessimistic attitudes. Our Lord would have us throw off the shackles that bind us to the defeated life, and move upward in triumph. Our Lord would raise up men and women who face the dilemmas of our time with faith and commitment.

I am aware that the apostle Paul asked in the Scripture: "And who is sufficient for these things?" (2 Cor. 2:16). But I also know that we cannot afford to falter every time we hit a snag.

Hasn't anyone ever heard of what happened to Jesus? How can we bring ourselves to whine and recline when we hear in the background the unmistakable sound of hammers pounding nails into a wooden cross?

So the going is tough. In God's name, what do we expect? To rough it smoothly?

Let us get up against the gospel, for it comes to us where we are. It holds out the glorious hope of staking our all on the blessed truth: "In all these things we are more than conquerors through him that loved us" (Rom. 8:37).

Who is sufficient for the living of these days? All who realize that their sufficiency is not of themselves but of Christ.

Almost ten years ago on a Sunday afternoon, I was sitting in my easy chair relaxing between the morning and evening worship services, when the phone rang and a long distance call reported that my parents had been in an automobile accident.

Not knowing any details, except that my parents had been driving up for a few days relaxation in the mountains of North Georgia, my wife and I jumped into my car and drove as quickly as we could from Athens to the Buford, Georgia, hospital.

Arriving there, I hurriedly parked the car, ran to the emergency room, and asked the nurse where I could find the Griffiths.

Pausing to look up from what she was doing, the nurse said, "They're at the funeral home."

"Both of them," I said.

"Yes, both of them," she said.

My parents had been horribly mangled and killed in a car-train collison.

It had been one of those blind railroad crossings, with no warning light and no automatic guardrail to halt traffic as trains approached. Mother was killed instantly and Dad had lived for about a half an hour following the accident.

My wife and I sat down in the waiting room to await

the arrival of my brother who was driving to the hospital from Macon, Georgia. In an hour he arrived, and I met him in the hall to say, "Ben, Mother and Daddy are in heaven."

He was stunned, as I had been. And he repeated the same question that I had asked: "Both of them?"

"Yes," I said, "both of them."

We moved over into a darkened corner of the hospital hall and shared our tears and our sorrow. But in a little while I said, "We will have to look where the folks always looked—to faith."

The next day we went back home to Macon for the double funeral service held in their church there. Both parents had been dedicated Christians and active in their church. Dad was a deacon, and he had been a Sunday School teacher for over thirty-five years. It was touching and heartwarming to see the members of both of their Sunday School classes gathered at the church entrance as an honorary escort as we entered for the service and departed for the cemetery.

The next day we began the painful task of going through their personal belongings.

Opening their Bibles, we found an old church bulletin with a printed questionnaire from their pastor asking that they write down what Christ meant to them.

My Dad had written in that scrawling manner of his: "I am sixty-eight years old—Jesus Christ is my security."

Mother, left-handed, had written in her familiar penmanship: "Jesus Christ means life itself to me."

And Jesus Christ must mean no less to any of us. He must be first in all things. He is our strength. He is our security. He is sufficient.

As the apostle Paul said, "In all these things," whatever

these things may be, "we are more than conquerors through him that loved us."

So, as we look at life through the eyes of faith, let us look to Christ. And as we come face to face with our Lord, we shall bow before him and sing with our lips and lives:

> My faith looks up to thee,
> Thou Lamb of Calvary,
> Savior Divine!
> Now hear me while I pray,
> Take all my guilt away,
> O let me from this day
> Be wholly thine!
>
> May thy rich grace impart
> Strength to my fainting heart,
> My zeal inspire;
> As thou hast died for me,
> O may my love to thee,
> Pure, warm and changless be,
> A living fire!
>
> While life's dark maze I tread,
> And griefs around me spread,
> Be thou my guide;
> Bid darkness turn to day,
> Wipe sorrow's tears away,
> Nor let me ever stray
> From thee aside.

6
You Can Live in a Large Room

Thou hast set my feet in a large room (Ps. 31:8).

In recent years, with the arrival of every daily newspaper and with each turn of the television dial, there came news of some new conquest of space.

But in a sense, the space race is as old as man himself. Man has always sought "more space—a broader, higher plane—on which to live."

The psalmist felt that he could better escape his enemies if he were allowed to dwell in a wide, open space.

For this blessing, he leaned upon God—for this blessing, he praised God.

"You have set my feet in a large room," he said (Ps. 31:8).

Of course, I am sure there are some who will say: "Well, that's easy enough for the psalmist to say—but that is not for me. I certainly do not live in a large room. The place I occupy in the world is a very small one."

But the truth the psalmist teaches here is that when we yield ourselves to God he so enlarges our vision and opportunity that we find ourselves in a different and larger world.

If the world has closed in on you, if you seem to be living in a small room, then Christ can change all that.

So often, as we all know, circumstances can put your life in a small room.

For example, here is a man who, in his youth, had thought of life as just one big adventure, a world of surprise and wonder. What happened? Instead he finds himself, after ten years, tied down to his daily task, his whole world packed and jammed into the narrow limits of his office or his workshop.

And think of his wife. Oh, how eagerly on her wedding day she had looked to the future. What happened? Now she finds that her whole existence is an endless round of cooking, sweeping, dusting, and caring for the everyday needs of her household.

They—both the husband and the wife—live in small rooms; their lives are surrounded by four walls. It is at times, to be sure, depressing. It is also nerve-racking.

An ambulance once made a rush call out into the country to a farmhouse where a woman had suddenly gone berserk. She had not hurt herself or anyone else, but it had so startled her husband that he had sent someone running off to find a telephone, place an urgent call to the proper authorities, and have his wife removed to a nearby institution.

The old man was stunned by what had happened. He couldn't figure it out. The doctor came and gave the woman something to quiet her and then took her away in the ambulance.

The old farmer sat in his rocking chair by the fire, rocking slowly and thinking. The doctor came in and told him that in order to better understand the woman's condition, he wanted to ask a few questions. He asked if the woman had ever had a spell like that before. "No, nary a time," the farmer replied.

"Has she ever seemed to act strangely in any way?" the doctor continued.

"Not as I can recall. I just don't know what happened," the old man declared, still bewildered.

"Well, can you think of anything that might have brought this on," the doctor persisted.

"No sir!" the farmer stated emphatically. "Why, Doc, she ain't been out of the kitchen in twenty-five years!"

The farmer's wife, it would seem, was living in a small room. She was living in a world that had closed in upon her.

What are we to do when life closes in upon us?

There are two ways in which we can enlarge a room, both of which have to do with a remodeling job. We can raise the ceiling or we can push back the walls. And Jesus Christ does both when he enters a life.

Christ transfigures life. He changes the form of life; he changes the appearance of life; he glorifies life; he expands and enlarges life.

It is said that once a poor artist used up all his canvas and had no funds with which to buy more.

A cook, trying to make a joke, tossed the artist a napkin and said, with a laugh, "Here great artist, paint on this."

The artist swallowed his pride, took the napkin, and painted upon it the beautiful face of the Madonna, a famous painting which is now known as the *Madonna of the Napkin.*

So Christ, the great artist, can take the most ordinary lives—he can take whatever is tossed at him—and make something out of them, giving unto them immortal beauty by creating them in his love and likeness.

In our daily work, Christ, if we take him into partnership, pushes back the walls and causes us to live in a larger world. Remember, it was Jesus himself who said, "I came that [you] may have life, and have it abundantly" (John 10:10, RSV).

A newspaper correspondent once said that he was on his way to fill a routine assignment. It was raining and he was tired and discouraged. Everything seemed so futile and meaningless.

Then someone told him a parable. A certain man saw

three workmen with their hammers and chisels cutting stones.

"What are you doing?" he asked one of them.

"I am chipping this bit of stone," he answered.

When the next man was asked, he replied: "Earning my living for myself and my family."

"And you, what are you doing?" he asked the third.

"Building a cathedral," was the answer.

To this workman, his daily task was a part of God's plan. Somehow that realization had pushed back the walls and admitted him into the larger room of God's universe.

When our lives are linked to God and his plan, we realize then that in this world we occupy not a small place, but a large place.

What a small place the average woman in the home thinks she fills in a busy world. But this is not a true picture.

We think of John Wesley as the founder of the Methodist Church, but in a sense, it was not he, but his mother, Susannah Wesley. She was the wife of a minister and there were 19 children in that tiny parsonage and only one woman's hands and heart to care for them all.

Could you imagine a smaller place for that stupendous task than a poor, cramped little cottage? But God was there and pushed out those walls till this great woman could see the ends of the earth.

As she held the baby Charles in her arms and sang him to sleep, she saw by faith this son of hers as one of the greatest hymn writers of all time whose songs will be sung as long as the Christian church endures.

As she taught her little John of God and truth, she could see by faith the untold millions who, through him, would seek and find God. Her place—her room was not a small room—but a large room—for God made it so.

And then, too, we are prone, in most instances, to feel that trouble and adversity can press life into a small room.

We forget that Christ and Christian faith can transform even this into a large place, for no place, no life, no soul can be small in which Christ lives.

I was asked one Sunday evening to preach at a beautiful church in a small Georgia town. I arrived late in the afternoon and after eating with the pastor and his wife, I was asked to go with the preacher on a visit before the evening service got underway.

While driving the short distance, the preacher said: "I want to tell you a little about this sick woman we are going to visit. She is critically ill. She is dying of cancer. The doctors have given up all hope for her. She has been in bed for a long, long time. But I want to tell you something else. Even in her condition she gives me more support, more strength than any other member in my church."

When we arrived at her home and went into her room, I saw immediately what he meant. It was true. She was dying of cancer, but was living for her Lord.

I told her I'd like to have a word of prayer with her and as I held her hand and prayed softly, I was the one who gained strength from God.

She was confined to one room for the rest of her life, but Jesus had come into that room, pushed out those four walls, raised the ceiling, and she was living in a large room.

No place can be small in which Christ lives, for even if the place is small, the soul can be large.

The psalmist said, "Thou hast set my feet in a large room" (Ps. 31:8).

Live for Christ; live with Christ; your life shall be lived in a large room, in the very largest, finest, fullest way!

7
You Can Keep Life's Appointments

Nevertheless, I must go on my way today and tomorrow and the day following (Luke 13:33, RSV).

Ever since Adam people have been saying, "The trouble with life is that it is so daily." Life is not only one day after another but it is also one thing after another.

There is a neat little wall plaque which features comforting, if not altogether true, words: "Life by the yard is hard, but life by the inch is a cinch." Actually, life when viewed from hindsight in large, comfortable blocks of time may be one thing, but frustrations frequently come when one tries to meet the day-by-day obligations and appointments.

Indeed, there are some who can readily identify with the sign which a busy executive has on his desk, "If you can keep your head while all those around you are losing theirs, then, brother, you simply don't understand the situation."

An office worker and busy mother, foundering in the pool of depression and fearing she was in danger of going down for the third time, came one day to my office. Caught in the throes of deep depression for which there seemed to be no real cause, she was struggling like someone caught in a giant spider web and trying desperately to pull herself away. It had become torture, she said, to keep her daily work schedule. Only with the understanding and loving assistance of her husband was she able to force herself into her car each morning for the drive to her office complex.

Her desire, with the dawning of each new day, was to

escape by remaining in bed not merely to sleep but to hide from the life she did not want to face.

In seeking professional assistance, she had been told that to win out over this problem she must face up to it and continue to do what had to be done from day to day. The victory would come not by avoiding but keeping life's appointment. She knew this. But like many others who face the same fight, this young woman had a definite need: the need to put on the whole armor of faith and take up her sword of determination before setting out again in the battle of life.

Late one afternoon, a man, fifty-five, obviously disturbed, rushed into the pastor's office. He was the bread-winner for a large family, with the added pressure of having two children in college at the same time. Pale-faced, hands shaking, he blurted out his own distress signal: "I just had to talk to you!"

His frantic words continued to pour out: "My sales supervisor is coming next week—he will be with me—breathing down my neck, examining everything I do, and criticizing every sale I try to make. I know he will be saying that I'm just getting too old to stay in the ball game. He will be thinking to himself, we need to bench this man and get us a younger, more aggressive salesman."

I waited until he had finished and then I calmly said: "As I remember, your supervisor came last year at about this same time, did he not?"

"Yes," he answered.

"And you made it through the week?" I asked.

"Yes," he said, "with God's help and your help."

"Well," I suggested, "the same help is available at this very moment."

"I know," he said, "and I know I've got to do this thing, and yet I feel that I can't. But I know I must."

We talked a few minutes longer, reflecting on God's Word and his promises, and then we prayed together—as I had with the schoolteacher. Shortly thereafter, he left with a new spring in his step, fortified in his faith.

It is good to report that in these instances the daily appointments with responsibility were kept by both the man and woman. They were strengthened by the Lord's presence and by the reminder that our Savior knew what it was to come to that decisive place where he said, "I must keep life's appointments. I must be on my way."

Certain Pharisees came to Jesus and said, "You had better move along. Go somewhere else. Herod will kill you."

Jesus replied, "Nevertheless, I must go on my way today and tomorrow and the day following." Our Lord was saying: "I have a rendezvous with life as well as with death; I shall keep them both. I have a duty to be done; I shall do it. I have service to render; I shall render it. I must keep life's appointments."

Our lives, too, have appointments. The words might also fall from our lips: "Nevertheless, I must go on my way today." Ours are personal appointments. My task is my task; it belongs to no other. My service is my service; it can be rendered by no one else.

As stinging as the accusation may be, it must be admitted that much of what we do comes under the heading of *sitting*. With more truth than they perhaps realize, there are people who boast that they have "sat under the ministry" of a certain pastor for many years. That just may be part of the trouble: we sit when we should stand. One wonders just how many problems would be solved and how many appointments would be kept by simply remembering the injunction: "Having done all, to stand" (Eph. 6:13, RSV).

When it comes to facing up to the requirements of life,

that person who is destined to have great difficulty is the *balk artist*. That's right—that's what I said, *balk artist*. He is not to be confused with the chalk artist. The fact is, the balk artist doesn't make a very pretty picture. As one might guess, he balks at almost everything. His transmission is used in only two ways: "for idling and stopping." His Bible is the Reversed Standard Version.

But our Lord never balked. Jesus made the choices that had to be made. Is the going tough? Are you depressed? Do you feel that no one appreciates you? In light of the hostility of the Pharisees, Jesus could feel all of these things. But his word was, "Nevertheless, I must go on my way today and tomorrow and the day following."

And so, too, must each of us make a choice. We must keep life's appointments. Life must be more than whim and chance. A person's dominant purpose in life determines the choice of appointments. All would do well to remember there are some things that deserve little place in life. There are other things that deserve no place at all.

Our Lord was concerned that we know of that which deserves first place in our lives. Jesus gives us a choice-pattern in these words, "Seek ye first the kingdom of God and His righteousness" (Matt. 6:33). This choice-pattern will determine life's appointments, and it will enable a person to realize his greatest possibilities and make his largest contribution to life. But more than this, by such a choice-pattern, you will know that your way is Christ's way. And by continuing in the way of Christ we have the sure path that leads to development of Christian character and fortitude.

It is by high choice and continuance in that choice that a life may be lived to the glory of God. Today's appointment is not tomorrow's, nor is tomorrow's today's. Grace is given to meet each day's needs when the day comes. The secret of continuance is meeting life a day at a time—today and then tomorrow and then the day after—all in the strength and the power of Jesus Christ.[1]

To know and to follow and always choose that which leads to a closer walk with Christ is to know the full meaning of the words in the Scripture: "As our days so shall our strength be" (Deut. 33:25, author's translation).

In the answer of Jesus to the Pharisees, there is another word suggested. It is the word, *compulsion*. "I must go on my way." There were *musts* in the life of Jesus and in the lives of his followers. Not to Jesus alone, but to every man, there comes the inevitable days of life. No human being can escape the necessity of saying at some hour, "I must."[2]

The word *must* is not one of the more popular words in our language. Before some, the word stands like a jagged rock of a cliff which they seek to avoid. But there comes a time when we cannot go around the word *must*; we cannot evade the compulsions of life.

If we are to have a safe voyage on the sea of life, we must seek our safety in the care and company of the Master Pilot, Jesus Christ. I have spent part of my life on the coast in two separate pastorates and I have learned some valuable lessons from the sea.

While serving as pastor on Saint Simons Island, Georgia, I talked once to an old and experienced harbor pilot who had guided many ships to a safe anchorage at the dock. He said that the only way to have a safe journey, on short and long trips, was to always keep the ship on the right course. So, too, must we keep ourselves in the mainstream of the will of God, where, through his Son Jesus, we may know the strength of his spirit, the direction of his wisdom, and the warmth of his love.

Moreover, we must keep moving on, despite the complications that come our way. "Nevertheless," Jesus said, "I must go my way." The word *nevertheless* indicates complication. Jesus had to keep life's appointments in the midst of complications. The Pharisees were hindering his work at every step. They were saying to Jesus, "You can't!" Herod was seeking to kill Jesus, but he had to go on his way.

Others have gone on their way in spite of complications which would hinder them. I recall that I instinctively liked a particular young man the first time I saw him. His warm smile began at his chin and covered his face. Strong arms were topped off by broad shoulders. It was only when he reached out for a friendly handshake that you became more aware that this act required the releasing of the hand strap on one of his crutches. Polio had left its mark from his waist down.

With skill and agility, he shuffled along from place to place, taking no thought of his problem. It was apparent that although God had not removed the braces from his legs, he had experienced the *healing* of having the braces removed from his mind. Oh it was known that he often had discomfort and pain, but this young man looked to his faith rather than his difficulties. Participating in all phases of his church's youth program, he asked no favors. He would do what everyone else would do.

I rejoiced with him at the surmounting of every obstacle. Getting through college was not easy. There were trying days. But he made it. Through every hardship, God was watching over him, speaking the encouraging words, Sure you can. When the invitation came to attend his college graduation, I stared at it for a long pleasant moment and gratefully fingered the engraved printing. Pastoral pride and joy started deep inside me, lumped in my throat, and moistened my eyes.

Following graduation, my young friend returned home

to his community. Commitment to Christ and the work of the church continued. He was elected a deacon by the congregation that had nurtured him and watched him grow up physically and spiritually.

Applying himself to his daily task, his hard work brought him success on the job. As a result, his firm named him "salesman of the year." What is his secret? Strong faith in Christ, tenacity, and the optimistic realization that life's dark complications can be tunnels through which we pass before coming out into the light of joy and achievement. In keeping life's appointments he said, "Nevertheless, with God's help, I must go on my way."

Admittedly, these are troubled times in which we live. Life does become complicated. We do live in the midst of perplexity. Confusion is the order of the day. We face great uncertainties. We know disappointments. But like the most precious jewel found in the darkest, dirtiest hole in the diamond mine, there is a glittering gem of truth here for all who would embrace the triumphant Christian faith. Our disappointment can be Christ's appointment for the bringing of new strength and power into our lives.

During a recent city-wide fund-raising drive for cancer research, solicitors were astonished to learn that the most determined and effective worker was a widow who had been blind for more than thirteen years.

This woman, however, saw nothing unusual in what she had done. "After all," she said, "I was taught to be self-reliant and I can distinguish between light and shadow, so I am not altogether helpless. And thank God, I never was one to be sad. There is much that I can do, and by God's grace I intend to do it."

Faithfully and victoriously, she was going on to keep her appointment with life. Blind? Yes. Older than some?

Yes. But, like Jesus, she was saying, "Nevertheless, I must go on my way today and tomorrow and the day following."

As a Christian, your appointment is to keep the faith and choose Christ's way for your life. Make your life an expression of dedication to the will and way of Christ. When this is done, it is possible to rise above the complications of life, not denying that they exist but meeting them with a firm, "Nevertheless, I must go on my way."

So then, let us go forward, as did Jesus, made steadfast and strong, in faith, in trustful reliance upon the loving God who gives to our hearts and lives the peace and strength that no one else can give.

8
The Secret of Security: Your Heart Fixed on God

He shall not be afraid of evil tidings: his heart is fixed, trusting in the Lord (Ps. 112:7).

Many of the books on first aid, which are in circulation today, insist that the best thing to do when you feel faint, is to stick your head between your knees.

As you assume this position, the feeling that you are about to faint is supposed to pass.

So far as I can determine, there is only one catch to this: If you are agile enough, and in good enough condition to perform the difficult feat of putting your head between your knees you are not likely to be bothered by fainting spells.

Still, there is an important spiritual lesson which can be learned from this advice on how to keep from fainting. When feeling faint in the physical sense, there may be some who stubbornly refuse to follow the first aid advice. But, oddly enough, when some people feel faint of mind and faint of spirit, they do just that. They tuck their heads and keep them hidden away like so many sick chickens seeking refuge under their own wings.

It is apparent that many persons living in this frantic and troubled age, though claiming to possess a relationship with the all-powerful, all-loving, and all-merciful God, have forgotten God's remedy for fainting.

The word *faint* in biblical terminology is very expressive. It means that not only our physical strength is gone, but that courage, hope, and spirit have departed also. Needless to say, there are many people who faint physically, but the most widespread affliction of fainting in today's hectic world is fainting spiritually.

One who faints spiritually is one whose heart becomes like water and who is helpless in the face of foes when he should be strong. He feels faint of spirit at the sight of trouble and faint of mind and heart when life pounces upon him.

For example, most of us are affected by the fear of bad news. If we think we are immune, we have only to recall the feeling that comes to us when someone hands us a telegram or we get an unexpected long distance phone call. We cannot avoid the shadow of anxiety. The fear of evil tidings is there lurking behind the mind. It springs from the feeling that this is an uncertain world where there is always the risk that mischance or misfortune may befall us.

It is certain that, at one time or another, many persons become weary, weak in the knees, troubled, and faint of mind and heart. But Christian faith and Christian assurance tell us that there is a marvelous remedy for spiritual fainting and we should make good use of God's smelling salts which are set down for us in great biblical passages such as Psalm 27.

Look with the eyes of your heart at Psalm 27:13: "I had fainted, unless I had believed to see the goodness of the Lord in the land of the living."

Without belief, without the assurance of courageous faith, there will be many who will faint in these demanding and distressing days.

The psalmist was expressing a truth that could be said of this very day, "I would have fainted unless I had believed in the goodness of the Lord in the land of the living" (author's translation).

When the odds against us are great, when the future is dark, and when everything appears on the futile side, it is belief "in the goodness of the Lord in the land of the living" that keeps us from fainting.

Darkness rolls in at times upon every life. It may come in for a short stay or it could establish residence for a long time. Trouble which tests our faith can come into our lives at any given second.

In my senior year at Southeastern Baptist Theological Seminary in Wake Forest, North Carolina, the alarm clock went off in my room on a Friday morning and beckoned me to shave and dress for my eight o'clock class.

I looked forward to Fridays. When my last class was over at noon, I would rush to the car for the drive home to see my wife and two small children who lived on the church field at North Myrtle Beach, South Carolina. I attended classes from Tuesday until Friday and then returned to serve my church on weekends. It was about 185 miles from my church to the seminary, and the miles seemed to go slowly every Friday as I eagerly returned home to be reunited with my family.

I was thinking of all this when I turned on the radio to get the early morning news and heard the astounding word that Hurricane Hazel was moving inland to the Atlantic Coast and was expected to make a direct hit on North Myrtle Beach, South Carolina, shortly after eight o'clock that morning.

The news was made even more frightening by the bulletin stating that winds of 120 miles an hour would be striking the coast and the little village where I lived at precisely high tide.

I skipped breakfast, located my fellow seminary student and traveling companion whose wife and children also stayed on his church field at Wampee, South Carolina, a few miles inland from the coast. We went to see our professor before the eight o'clock class was scheduled to begin.

He understood our anxiety when we told him that we felt we must leave for home as quickly as possible. We were worried about our wives and our children who could be caught in the fury of the storm. He excused us from class and told us to go with the assurance that he and the members of the class would be praying for us and our families. As we reached the car and started the trip to the coast, the lines of communication were already down. It was impossible to get a telephone call through. I held on to the hope that my wife and children had been evacuated across the bridge, before it was too late.

We drove on, trying to pick up news from the radio, praying all the while, and hoping for the best. After we had gone about 50 miles, the radio announcer said: "Winds of 120 miles an hour had made a direct hit at North Myrtle Beach at high tide that morning.

"Tidal waves rising to some 30 feet in height had engulfed the little community, covering the store buildings along the water front, flooding the streets, and even going over the top of electric light poles."

The home provided for us by my church was located a few blocks from the beach. My friend was comforted in that no loss of homes, serious damage nor injuries had been reported at points inland. Not so with me.

If not hopeless, it was a helpless feeling. Here we were over 130 miles from the coast with no word about my family—my wife and two little girls—and the reports coming from the coast were about as bad as they could be. We prayed and we trusted and we kept our heart fixed on God.

The high winds were now moving toward us and blowing directly across our path as we tried to make our way to the coast. Trees had fallen all along the road and telephone and power lines were down. Frequently, my friend stopped the car and I would get out and guide the driver around a fallen tree. It was becoming more difficult with each passing moment to keep the car on the road. The small, light car became a plaything of the wind.

As we drove on, some seventy-five miles from our destination, we neared a small North Carolina town when a strong gust of wind picked up the car and slid it into the ditch on the side of the road. The pouring rain drenched us as we pulled ourselves out of the car, surveyed the situation, and were relieved to discover that we were unhurt and that the car was not seriously damaged.

Hiking to a small country store that we could see in the distance, we hoped to find a phone that was still in operation and someone who could pull us out of the ditch. The storekeeper suggested a man who had a tow truck and gave us his number. The call was placed and a friendly but anxious voice on the other end of the line said, "I'll be glad to come out and help you as soon as I can, but the wind just blew the roof off my house."

Hurricane Hazel was asserting her power in no uncertain terms. With all lines down on the coast and unable to call home, we sat down and awaited the arrival of our good Samaritan with the tow truck.

But we also waited on another Friend. After all, the Scripture says, "Wait on the Lord: be of good courage, and he shall strengthen thine heart" (Ps. 27:14).

As we were pulled back onto the highway and resumed our journey, trees were down everywhere. Hurricane Hazel had been no lady. Surveying the damage all along the road, we rubbed our eyes in unbelief.

However, the greatest shock awaited our arrival on the coast. The damage was startling. Beautiful, sturdy homes along the beach had been washed out to sea. Hotels and motels along the ocean front had been leveled. Many people who had been evacuated across the bridge returned to their homes to find nothing remaining but the lot on which the house had stood. Personal belongings and possessions were gone.

Driving to my home, still in doubt about the safety of my family, I was relieved to see that the house still stood. Jumping out of the car I rushed to my wife who was equally relieved to see me. Breathing a prayer of gratitude, I threw my arms around her and my two small children. It was one of the happiest family reunions I have ever attended. They had spent the night in a schoolhouse located eight miles inland.

Miraculously, no lives were lost in the storm, but the property damage and loss amounted to millions of dollars along the beach front. Losses were so severe that it was feared that some would never recover financially. Some homes would not be built back.

That night I went to see as many people as I could to bring whatever comfort possible.

On Saturday morning I resumed my pastoral visitation, going from homesite to homesite, trying to locate people who were devastated by their losses. I saw people who had been extremely wealthy, now down, crawling on their knees digging in the sand, hoping to find pieces of family silver.

I saw many others now homeless—without clothes, food, or any personal conveniences.

As I stood amidst the ruins, the truth of the Bible spoke to me in a vivid way: "And this word, Yet once more, signifieth the removing of those things that are shaken, as of things that are made, that those things which cannot be shaken may remain" (Heb. 12:27).

Sunday morning we gathered for services at our little church building which had been untouched by the storm. With borrowed clothes and hitched rides—since many automobiles had been swept out to sea—my little congregation came together for worship. The people were red-eyed, shocked, stunned with grief and loss. Some were like a defeated boxer who has suffered so many quick and surprising blows that he now hangs on the ropes—beaten and on the verge of going down for the last count.

God, at this moment, gave me the text from which he wanted me to preach: "I had fainted, unless I had believed to see the goodness of the Lord in the land of the living" (Ps. 27:13). There was a silence that you could almost hear as the words were read. God spoke through his Word. God said what these discouraged and dejected people needed to hear. I tried to preach, to tell these friends that we had to look beyond the destruction, beyond the discouragement, beyond the disappointment, and slip our hands into the hand of the Lord and to let him lead us one step at a time.

I said this to men who two days before had fine wardrobes and beautiful homes—men who now did not have a suit of clothes. I reminded them of the other word of the psalmist: "He shall not be afraid of evil tidings: his heart is fixed, trusting in the Lord" (112:7). The words of God brought comfort to those dazed and distressed friends. This is the secret of security—a heart fixed on God, a heart trusting in the Lord.

An eminent Christian once said that he was never afraid of bad news because his heart was fixed on God. He was not afraid because he was trusting in the Lord.

In a hurricane or any other horrible experience, the secret of security is a heart fixed on God. If our hearts are fixed, trusting in the Lord, he will take possession of our lives disturbed, discouraged, or devastated as they may be. If our hand grips the hand of God, he will take hold of our hand. There is, within the heart of the surrendered

Christian, the knowledge that whatever he has to meet, God will see him through. God has the power to meet any situation. For whatever changes may come, God does not change and his grace is sufficient.

A preacher once told of a visit which he enjoyed with some friends out West. They were warm and hospitable friends and wanted to make him comfortable in every way. In the room where he slept the bedcover was made out of old brown linen that had been spun in the old days by a godly grandmother. Over it she had worked with her needle the lines:

> God's greatness flows around our incompleteness
> Around our restlessness is His rest.

When asked the next morning how he had slept, the preacher said, "How could I have slept other than well with such a text as that on top of me?"

This is the secret of the peace which the world cannot give, and which it cannot take away: God is changeless.

"Jesus Christ the same yesterday, and today, and forever" (Heb. 13:8).

Furthermore, the heart fixed on the Lord has another secret of security. When our hearts are set on God and on his purpose, we discover the real treasures of life. We know that these cannot be touched by its changes and chances.

My friends along the South Carolina coast who felt that they had lost everything had a new understanding of the words of Jesus: "Lay not up for yourselves treasures upon earth, where moth and rust doth corrupt, and where thieves break through and steal: But lay up for yourselves treasures in heaven, where neither moth nor rust doth corrupt, and where thieves do not break through nor steal:

For where your treasure is, there will your heart be also"
(Matt. 6:19–21).

Jesus warned us that we are living in an uncertain world.
If our treasures are in possessions or things on which many
people set their hearts, we have no real security from fear.
"Moth and rust do corrupt. Thieves do break through and
steal."

In the terrible destruction brought by the hurricane,
one could see how easily *things* could be swept away.
Houses were gone and lots had to be resurveyed along the
beach to find property lines. Expensive automobiles, costly
clothing, valuable family heirlooms—all these things were
either swept away or buried in the sand along the beach.

The only way of security is to set your heart on the
things which cannot be shaken by the most tragic events of
time. When your heart is fixed and you trust in the Lord,
this can be your way of victorious faith.

In the weeks and months after Hurricane Hazel, I spent
a great deal of my pastoral time in attempting to encourage
and to bolster my people—to tell them that they could.
They could come back. They could build back. They
could survive. They could start over and rebuild their
homes and their businesses. Much of my time was spent in
offering prayer and encouragement to members of my
congregation, with the much-needed words: *You can.*

During those days, when I was reaching down into the
very depths of my soul to bring up as much strength as I
could possibly summon forth, I reflected many times on the
wonderful faith of my grandmother—my mother's mother.
This little lady, scarcely five feet tall, was a tower of Christian faith. When I was a small boy, she had great influence
on my Christian life. She was so entwined in the spirit of
Christ and in the love of Christ and in the strength of

Christ that nothing seemed to set her back. She walked by faith and lived by faith. There was in her life such a closeness to God that to be with her was to be with one who was on the closest terms with almighty God.

She was not afraid of evil tidings; her heart was fixed; she trusted in the Lord. When the banks failed during the Depression and she lost a large sum of money, she did not despair. She took the loss with the greatest grace and the strongest faith. "It was only money," she said. Her treasures were in heaven.

No matter what the day brought, the beginning of each day would find her on her knees in prayer and the end of each day would find her saying good night to God in prayer. And without fail, she spent time in God's Word both morning and night.

She had a good and uplifting word for everyone. She knew how to encourage the discouraged, how to give new heart to the helpless.

All of her grandchildren, as well as everyone else, loved her very much. It was a kind of special joy to be around her. A small lad, not yet out of the Primary department of my Sunday School, I sat at her feet while she read the Bible. As the years went on and she became older and her eyes became dim, I noticed that it was becoming more difficult for her to read. She held the large-print Bible very close to her eyes.

One night I heard my parents talking. There was something wrong with grandmother's eyes. They planned to take her to an eye specialist the next day. She was now a very old woman and had other assorted ailments: some heart trouble, high blood pressure, and a touch of arthritis.

We went to the city nearby, her eyes were examined, and we were headed home late in the afternoon. Everyone was unusually quiet. The doctor's diagnosis had not been good. Grandmother was gradually losing her sight, and there was very little that could be done about it.

Saddened at the news, I did not want to think about it. I hardly knew what to say. Finally, I turned to this dear old lady and said, "Grandmother, I am sorry about your eyes."

Sitting next to me, she reached down, took my hand and said. "Why, Jim, that's all right. I'll be able to see everything I need to see. THE LORD WRITES LARGE!"

The truth of her statement has been revealed to me time after time through the years. Through trial and turmoil, through difficult days and hard years, I have remembered that the Lord does write large. And his word to us is that when we are yielded to his purpose and plan, we possess a security that cannot be threatened by accident or evil.

And no matter what may come our way—whether it be disaster or catastrophe—we do not have to faint, we can believe and see "the goodness of the Lord in the land of the living."

We can get up and try it over again. Although we can be knocked down, we do not have to stay down. We can bounce back.

What is the secret of security? It is simply this: "He shall not be afraid of evil tidings: his heart is fixed, trusting in the Lord."

9
Making a Picnic Out of Your Life

And Jesus said, Make the men sit down. Now there was much grass in the place. So the men sat down, in number about five thousand. And Jesus took the loaves; and when he had given thanks, he distributed to the disciples, and the disciples to them that were sat down; and likewise of the fishes as much as they would (John 6:10–11).

This miraculous scene painted by the Scripture pulls back the curtain of faith and reveals the most successful picnic the world has ever known.

The details are astonishing. It seems that a young boy out for the day, joined in the popular excitement caused by the wonderful Teacher and Healer named Jesus. The lad had a very moderate ration of five loaves and two fishes and yet we are told that Jesus took this light lunch and fed at least five thousand hungry persons.

The miracle of it! Five thousand and more hungry mouths fed with five hunks of bread and two pickled fish!

At this point you may be saying, "Here it comes—another discourse on miracles." You may even continue to say: "Certainly the feeding of five thousand and more persons was a miracle, but, after all, that was a very long time ago. No one believes in miracles anymore."

Well now, don't they! Perhaps you need to run that assumption through your thought processes one more time, for the fact is, there are multitudes all over the face of the earth who can tell us about miracles.

There are people around the world who would join me in the claim that there are powers we have not yet generally used—powers readily available to us and offered to us from the generous hands of our loving Savior. When used correctly and in accordance with the plan and purpose of

Christ for our lives, these powers can produce something out of this world.

The truth is, God is still working miracles and would work them in us and through us if we would completely surrender ourselves to the will and way of his son, Jesus.

It is distressing to observe that there are many persons today who have lost the hope that anything wonderful may happen to deliver them from the bondage and futility of life. They are bitter, irritable, and difficult to live with. Life, they think, has soured on them and they in turn have soured on life. They have become cold, hard, and cynical. They do not trust anyone.

A case in point was the dear old lady who badly needed twenty-five dollars. Seeking a remedy for her plight, she sat down and wrote a letter to God. Not knowing God's exact mailing address, she sent her letter in care of the postmaster.

As he read a moving and pathetic story describing the poor old woman's need of financial assistance, the postmaster's heart was touched. He went back into the mail distribution room, told the clerks of the need, passed the hat, and collected fifteen dollars which he put in an envelope and sent back to the old lady's return address.

A week went by and another letter addressed to: "The Lord in Heaven" arrived and was opened by the postmaster. Just as he had suspected, the letter was from the same source. With a warm feeling in his heart and the high hope that the money collected had been of great assistance to this needy person, he eagerly read the text of the letter. But the words were more amazing than amusing:

"Please, dear God, thank you for your assistance. I asked for twenty-five dollars and received only fifteen dollars. I suppose you sent the other ten. But next time, will you send it by registered mail, for you just can't trust those people in the post office."

More people than we care to imagine are like this old woman. They are bitter and untrusting. They are quite ready to bite the hand that feeds them. And this should not be. The marvelous story from the Scripture tells of a wonderful picnic. But life is not always a picnic some say. They are quick to complain that things just do not go that well.

Although it was a number of years ago, I can vividly remember a scene from that delightful motion picture, *Cheaper by the Dozen*. In this particular episode, the harassed father of twelve children was taking his entire brood for an automobile ride.

The ancient automobile in which they were riding was huffing, puffing, and straining under the heavy load and the father was making a supreme effort to keep his patience as his children began to fight, fuss, scuffle, and argue one with another.

He approached an intersection and slowed down to stop. Standing on the corner, a man observed the twelve passengers and all the commotion and asked with a smile: "Going on a picnic?"

The fuming father, his patience worn thin, answered, "Sir, all twelve of these children are mine, and believe me —it is no picnic!"

It is well within the mark to say that there are countless others who share his opinion that amidst all the problems and confusion of our age life is no picnic. And yet, these are questions we must ask ourselves: Why is this so? Why should it be this way? Here we are with a prevailing hunger for satisfaction, for the abundant life of happiness, and still we are faced with what many consider as impossible problems.

What is the answer to it all? I will tell you what I think is the only answer to the predicaments of life and it is simply this: The only thing that can rescue us from our quandary is a miracle—the miracle of Jesus Christ at work in our lives.

The Master took five thousand people, five loaves of bread, and two fish and made a picnic out of it. Faith declares that in the same way he can take you and your problems and make a picnic out of your life.

Look once again at the account of the boy and his picnic lunch. Jesus did not perform a miracle for the mere fun of it. It was not just a little bit of magic or for his own relief.

He and his disciples badly needed a break in their tiring schedule, and they had come to this out of the way bit of country for a rest, but the people still came crowding in upon the Master. As was so characteristic of Jesus, he was not annoyed. He was concerned for the needs of the multitude. He had compassion on them—he felt for them and with them.

Through the eyes of little faith the problem would seem to be insurmountable. All those mouths to feed! Five thousand men, plus the women and children! Have you ever seen an anxious, hungry crowd? You know what happens to even the best of children when they are hungry, and you also know the usual reaction that takes place with their parents. There can be no peace and quiet if a hungry child is around. Five thousand plus! That was the situation Jesus faced. A crowd with an urgent need. And Jesus fulfilled that need.

It is a marvelous story and it is a story that has a wonderful lesson for us. And the lesson is this: Jesus can make a picnic out of our lives if we, like the boy with the lunch, will do at least two things.

First, we must offer our humble best to Christ, even

though seemingly it is of little value. It is the first step on the road to solution to both small and large problems.

After we had detonated our first atomic bomb in New Mexico, Herman Hagedorn wrote these words:

> I went to call on the Lord in His
>   house on the high hill,
> My head full of one hundred and fifty
>   million people who had to grow up overnight.
> "If ever a people, Lord, needed a
>   miracle!" I said.
> The Lord He looked at me as a
>   mountain might look at a molecule.
> "So you want a miracle," said the
>   Lord. "My! My! You want a miracle!
> I suppose you mean you want me to
>   come sliding down a sunbeam and
>   make one hundred and fifty million
>   self-willed egotists overnight into
>   one hundred and fifty million co-
>   operative angels?
> "Brother," said the Lord, in a voice
>   that shook the windows, "that is
>   not the sort of universe you are
>   living in.
> And that isn't the sort of God I am."
> First, give me your life, and this day it
>   shall be like a new world.
> The unclean shall be clean, the cowardly,
>   courageous, and the weak, powerful." [1]

In any event of life, offering our humble best to the Lord is still the answer. The lad with the lunch gave Jesus the best that he had and all that he had. It seemed a very little bit in the midst of five thousand and more hungry people. Perhaps he was a little ashamed of it, but he gave it—gave all that he had—and Jesus used it to feed the multitude.

I shall never forget the day I surrendered to God's call to be a minister. For more than seven years I had worked as a newspaper man, and I had received my college degree in journalism. I was then editor of a newspaper in a North Carolina city. But God had other plans.

After much soul-searching and many sleepless nights, my wife and I surrendered to the highest calling.

I wrote my parents and told them that I had fought this call of God long enough. "Although I feel totally unprepared and completely unworthy to be one of God's ministers, I have reached the point where I must preach," I said.

Several days later I received a letter from my father and it contained some of the best advice I have ever received.

"You say, Son," he said, "that you feel completely unworthy for the ministry. It is good to feel humble, but there is one thing I hope you will never forget. I want you to always remember the story in the Bible of the boy who had only five loaves and two fishes. That was all he had. But he gave all that he had to Jesus and the Master did the rest."

This is the blueprint for the working of any miracle by the Lord in our lives. If it is our desire that something wonderful take place in our lives, we must be ready, willing, and able to offer Jesus our humble best.

I like the spirit displayed by a Southern recipient of an army draft questionnaire who, after struggling with the long list of questions, gave up in despair and returned the blank form to his draft board with this notation: "I is ready when you is."

What a wonderful thing it would be if we were just as ready and willing to offer ourselves to Jesus, for that is the first requirement if he is to perform a miracle and make a picnic out of our lives.

The second thing we must do, after giving Jesus the best

that we have, is to trust him to bless and use what we have given him, inadequate though we may consider it to be.

I should imagine that the young lad was amazed beyond words when one of the disciples of Jesus came to him and said, "The Master needs your lunch."

"Needs my lunch," the boy said, "for what?"

"He is going to feed the multitude," the disciple said.

"You mean," said the boy, "he is going to take my five loaves and two fish and feed all of these people!"

"That is right," said the disciple, "we must trust him. Give him your lunch and trust him for the results."

The boy did just that. And as a result all were fed.

Christians of all the ages will testify that if we do our part and trust in the Lord, he will bless our efforts. One of the most unforgettable characters I have ever met was a favorite aunt of mine who lived out this truth in her daily life. Aunt Emmie practiced faith in God and the fine art of positive thinking and positive living in all that she did. And she did so, despite hardship and trouble of almost every description. Her husband, a young man of brilliant mind and bright promise, was struck by a car in early manhood. He was disabled by the accident and unable to work at a regular job.

Circumstances dictated that Aunt Emmie become the inspirational leader of her brood which included five children, two girls and three boys. With water in the soup, faith in her heart, and a smile always on her lips, she held things together with the cement of affirmation. "We will do the best we can," she said, "and trust in the Lord."

As her children grew older and left the nest to attain success in various fields, she continued, in her marvelous way, to believe that life was good and getting better. Aunt Emmie was a living confirmation of the words of Aeschylus, first of the great ancient Greek dramatists who declared: "Happiness comes from the health of the soul." [2]

In spite of long years of toil and trouble, this sturdy and courageous and faithful woman affirmed with her life that to have health of soul one must practice joyous daily thanksgiving. She appreciated God's world and gave thanks daily for her personal blessings. Her unofficial motto was: Think happy thoughts and do things that make other people happy.

Even when she reached her eighties, Aunt Emmie maintained that "the older she got the better she felt." One Sunday morning she went to her Sunday School class, made up of women who were eighty years old and above. As she sat down to begin the class, she announced to all the other class members that she had come to the conclusion that "the older you get the better you feel."

A little old lady of ninety looked her straight in the eye, winked and said, "Honey, when I get old, I will let you know!"

Aunt Emmie rejoiced that she had obviously found another person who always looked on the positive side.

My aunt was somewhat like the widow who had been left with six sons to bring up and was asked one day how she had managed to raise such exceptional sons alone and unaided.

"It did take grit and grace," she said, "but I wasn't exactly unaided—the good Lord helped me. Every night I knelt in prayer and told him I would furnish the grit if he would furnish the grace."

Often we are prone to forget that God can make the difference between defeat and victory in our lives. We forget that God is near and anxious to meet our need.

One afternoon a small boy was trying to lift a heavy stone, but he could not budge it. His father came in from work, strolled up the driveway, and stopped to watch his efforts. In a moment, he said to his son, "Boy, are you using all your strength?"

Exasperated, the boy cried, "Yes, I am."

"No, Son," the father said calmly. "You are not using all your strength—you haven't asked me to help you."

The truth is, we have not used all of our strength until we call upon our Father in heaven to assist us.

The lad with the five loaves and two fish faced an impossible situation, but he discovered that with the Lord's miraculous help nothing is impossible.

And Jesus can make a picnic out of your life—if you will bring him the best that you have, call upon him for help, and trust him with the final results.

10
You Can Trust in God's Everlasting Arms

And we know that all things work together for good to them that love God, to them who are the called according to his purpose (Rom. 8:28).

Do all things work together for good?

Can you trust in God's everlasting arms? One glance at our world through the columns of today's newspapers and we might say that nothing seems to work together according to any sort of plan.

And so we come again to the question: Do all things work together for good? In the light of daily disasters and catastrophes, where does one stand as he looks across a sea of tears and seeks to answer this question: Do all things work together for good?

It is obvious that the only way we can possibly accept the proposition that "all things work together for good" is to take all of the statement in this great Scripture. We must receive the verse in its entirety—not part of it. A superficial world, which does not wish to face up to the hard facts of sorrow and tragedy, leaps at the first part of the statement in its eagerness to assure itself that everything happens for the best.

As is so often the case, there are people who, for want of a better explanation, dismiss almost every tragic event in life with the cover-all statement: "All things work together for good. . . ." But we cannot stop there. Only a half-truth is stated at this point. The remainder of the Scriptural truth is: ". . . to them that love God and are the called according to his purpose."

Of course, it can be said that all things happen to all.

And it can also be said that even in the smallest mishap, there are some persons, like Chicken Little the familiar character in the children's story, who are certain that the sky is falling. This little chicken, you recall, was struck by a small pebble falling from the roof and immediately assumed that the sky was falling. So convinced was she of impending doom that she ran off to tell the king.[1]

Chicken Little is not the only one who has reacted in this way to trouble—whether it be real or imaginary. But this is not God's desired reaction for his children. Our Lord would have us live with confidence and calm assurance in good times and bad.

Has it ever occurred to you that almost everything happened to the apostle who was led to write the verse which speaks of "all things working together for good"? Paul was arrested, he was stoned, he was thrown into prison, he was flogged, he was shipwrecked, he was cast out of a city and left for dead. Yet, he used all these things to strengthen his own character, deepen his faith, and glorify his Lord. We find him saying with quiet confidence: "But I would ye should understand, brethren, that the things which happened unto me have fallen out rather unto the furtherance of the gospel" (Phil. 1:12).

How can it be that one man looks on shipwreck, arrest, stoning, and opposition as disaster while another looks upon these troubles as means of progress? The answer is in the man himself. Underneath the apostle Paul and his problems were the everlasting arms of God. The power and purpose of Christ was so much a part of Paul—Christ was so alive in him—that Paul was enabled to use all things for good.

Make no mistake about it. All things happen to us all: the laughter and tears, joy and sorrow, birth and death, health and sickness, success and failure. What these things do to us is determined by what we have inside of us. Developing this quality of character is no dark mystery which only a few can know. It is, indeed, very simple. Building up over the years a storehouse of faith upon which we can draw in time of need, walking with Christ every hour of every day—these are means of grace which enable us to endure whatever comes our way.

In every crisis of life, the person of genuine Christian faith is upheld by God's everlasting arms. Some years ago, my wife, Mimi, entered the hospital for major surgery. The surgery was successful and in ten days she was dismissed from the hospital. The three small children and I rejoiced to have Mother at home again. Even though at first she was unable to resume her regular duties as the chief lady of the pastorium, she could at least supervise and the children knew this would mean better meals and a smoother operation of the home front.

But something was wrong. She was not regaining her strength as had been anticipated. In fact, she grew weaker with each passing day. The doctor was consulted, but he tried to reassure us by saying that it was probably a delayed reaction to the surgery.

A week passed. She was now weaker than she had been on the day she came home from the hospital. Unable to get out of bed, her general condition had worsened.

The doctor thought it best that she return to the hospital for tests. At first, there was nothing conclusive except that with each passing day her condition became more serious.

In an attempt to meet the many demands of a busy pastorate and also spend as much time as I could at the hospital, I operated on a daily schedule which ran from 6 A.M. to 1 A.M. I experienced once again the spiritual truth: Where strength is needed, strength will be supplied. Fixing meals for the children, getting them off to school, running from the church office to the hospital, I was caught in a whirlpool of frenzied activity. But God was there. Each morning when the alarm went off at six, I would say: "Lord, here we go again! Be with my wife, my children, and me in every need of this day."

And each night, when I would finally get to bed, I would say: "Lord, I thank you that you've been with us through this day and that you are always with us to sustain and uphold us."

After more hospital tests, my wife's illness was diagnosed as serum hepatitis. The doctor, when he came to the room, gave it to us straight: She had suffered massive liver damage and was in critical condition.

With each passing day Mimi grew worse. As I greeted her early each morning, it was apparent that she was weaker than she had been the day before.

The wonderful people who made up our church fellowship were deeply concerned. Prayers were being offered throughout the community. Family members in distant places had been notified of the seriousness of her condition.

Then, a few nights later, God stepped in. As usual, I reached the hospital early in the morning. When I saw her, I knew that something wonderful had happened. There had been a dramatic change for the better.

Mimi explained it this way: "I had a long talk with God last night. I said, 'Lord, you know I'd like to get well. I have three small children and a husband. They need me. But Lord, whatever you want to do, it's all right with me. No matter what happens, I'm in your hands.' "

She said, from that moment on, she knew that she was being held in the everlasting arms of God. Complete recovery followed. This time our little lady came home from the hospital to stay.

Members of the Griffith household now had a new understanding of the scriptural promises of God as translated by Moffatt: "We know also that those who love God, those who have been called in terms of his purpose, have his aid and interest in everything" [2] (Rom. 8:28).

Underline in your mind and heart these words: "have his aid and interest in everything." This means that God is on our side in every struggle in which we are engaged. And "if God be for us, who can be against us?" (Rom. 8:31).

Admittedly, the pathway of tears is a common lot of mankind. All up and down the whole creation there is strife, strain, struggle for existence, pain, and death. Man cannot escape it. But man can meet it with a song in his heart. He cannot avoid it but he can, in Christ, surmount it.

A deacon who served with me in an earlier pastorate comes to mind. He was a faithful Christian who had three great loves in life: his Lord, his church, and his family. A conductor on the railroad, he was out of town for an overnight run when his house burned and all of his family's possessions were lost. His wife and children escaped injury, but they were crushed at the great loss of their home and belongings.

With clothes borrowed and pieced together from friends and neighbors, they dressed and drove to the railroad station to meet this faithful father and husband who knew nothing of the fire and the loss of his home and personal treasures.

When he got off the train, they rushed to him—two little girls and his wife—with the children crying out: "Oh, Daddy, something terrible has happened!" Looking at his wife and children with great love in his eyes, he said: "Oh, it couldn't be too bad—I still have all of you—you are here —and I have my faith in God."

A man with this kind of attitude of love and faith will prevail. He will stand in the midst of misfortune because he knows that his life is not subject to mere circumstances. He is upheld by the everlasting arms of God, sustained by a power above and beyond himself, guided by a hand not his own.

All experiences are included in the declaration of triumphant faith that insists: "All things work together for good to them that love God." Do not overlook the prerequisite: loving God. Goodspeed translates it: "We know that in everything God works with those who love Him." [3]

Look again at the entire verse: "And we know that all things work together for good to them that love God, to them that are the called according to his purpose." If we are centered in the will of God, then we know his purpose and love him in such a way that we take anything that befalls us and make it work out for good.

In the Old Testament you will find a man such as Joseph who was sold into slavery by his brothers, lied about by his master's wife, and thrown into jail. But as a result of being in jail, he explained the king's dream, was made prime minister, and thus was in a position of power and able to supply food to his brothers when famine sent them down to Egypt.

And so, when Paul sat down with pen in hand to write his letter to the Romans and tell them that "all things work together for good to those that love God," I can imagine Joseph looking over the banisters of heaven and sounding off with a hearty "Amen." Joseph would be quick to say that we have only to take the leap of faith to know that "all things do work together for good to them that love God,"—but we shall never know until we have taken the leap of faith.

The late headmaster of a certain academy used to take his little girl out to the school grounds in the late afternoon and place her on the ledge of one of the dining hall windows six feet from the ground. As he stood immediately below her, he would tell her to jump.

"Daddy," she would cry, "I can't."

"Oh, yes you can," was the father's invariable reply. "When you jump, my arms will be there."

Whatever else is uncertain in this world, this is certain and on this we can stake our lives: Underneath us—through every trial—there will be the arms of a loving heavenly Father to keep us from falling as we make the leap of faith.

We do not have to say, "we hope," or "think maybe," or "perhaps." We can join in the hallelujah chorus with the words of the Scripture: "We know!" In truth, we are positive, sure. We know that "all things work together for good to them that love God, to them who are the called according to his purpose." Phillips declares: "Moreover we know that to those who love God, who are called according to his plan, everything that happens fits into a pattern of good." [4]

It is possible for us to put these words to a test. This truth can be taken into the laboratory of life and demonstrated. The first step in the experiment is to fulfill the conditions of God. Complete surrender must be followed by obedience to our loving Lord.

As guidance from Christ comes it must be followed. As faith is born it must be nurtured. As trouble comes it must be immersed in the love of Christ.

As the experience—whether it be sorrow, or pain, or death, or failure—emerges in the light of God's love for us and our love for him, it begins to take on a hue which gives it a different, brighter color.

Worked into the fabric of life is the thought that God is weaving a pattern, a design in our lives. Viewed from our side, there is no clear-cut design but we know that from

God's side, there is a pattern which is plain to him. "Now we see through a glass darkly" (1 Cor. 13:12), but there will come a day when the mists will blow away and all will be clear.

The first church I served after finishing seminary was located in a small countyseat town in Georgia. One morning as I sat in my study at the church, I received an emergency phone call. The distressed voice on the other end of the line reported tragic news.

On the highway a few miles outside of town a head-on collision between a car and a truck had instantly brought death to a young newly-married couple in our community.

The young woman was a member of my church and only two months before I had officiated at her marriage ceremony. Now, both the bride and groom were dead. As rapidly as I could, I drove to the home of the young woman's parents, hoping to bring what comfort I could. Never, in my brief experience, had I seen people in such a terrible state of shock. They held on to only one thought: In a fleeting second, two young lives of high hope and promise had been wiped out.

It was not easy to speak to that mother about a God of love. The great wound in her heart could not be healed by some plaster of pious platitude. There was no neat little philosophical formula—there was no fine spun theological theory with which to banish this mother's bewilderment and ease her sorrow.

Desperately, I reached out for the Lord, the ultimate source of strength. He was the only one who could hold that distracted soul steady in her hour of agony. And I reminded that grief-stricken mother of Michael Bruce's moving lines:

> In every pang that rends the heart
> The Man of Sorrows has a part:

He sympathizes with our grief
And to the sufferer sends relief.

Only the understanding, sympathizing Savior who reached out his arms to this woman could ease her grief.

It was a tragedy that shook the entire community. In conducting the funeral service, I tried to bring comfort to both families who had suffered this devastating loss by telling them a story of a mine disaster that had taken place some years ago in which forty miners lost their lives. When the families of the men gathered about the entrance to the mine, struggling with sorrow and perplexity, someone asked a local minister to say something that would, in some way, help those people.

This is what he said: "We stand today in the midst of mystery, but I want to tell you about something I have at home. It is a bookmark, embroidered in silk by my mother and given to me many years ago. On one side the threads are crossed and recrossed in wild confusion. And looking at it, you would think that it had been done by someone with no idea of what she was doing. But when I turn it over, I see the words beautifully worked in silken threads to read: 'God is love.' "

"Now," he said, "we are looking at this tragedy from one side, and it does not make too much sense. Someday we shall be permitted to read its meaning from the other side. Meanwhile, let us wait and trust."

Continuing to speak in the funeral service, I said, "Here is what I want you to do: Wait for God's ultimate explanation and trust in your heavenly Father. For in all things we are certain that God is love. So let us have unfailing faith in the everlasting arms of God."

In spite of all that happens to each of us—tragedy, heartbreak, illness, and misfortune—we must trust and declare, once and for all: "We know that all things work together for good to them that love God, to them that are the called according to his purpose."

An outstanding college football player, who found his greatest joy in being a winning Christian, confirms this truth in a prayer which he composed:

Dear God: Help me to play well the game of life. I do not ask for any special place in the lineup; play me where you need me.

If all the hard drives come my way, I thank you for the compliment and your belief in my ability to take it. Help me take the bad breaks as part of the game.

Finally, if fate seems to hand me a bad deal, and I'm laid up in sickness or injury, help me to accept that part of the game, also.

Please help me not to whimper or complain, claiming that I have gotten a raw deal.

And when, at last, I hear the final gun, I ask for no great honors. I only want to know that you are pleased and that the game has been yours.

With God, all things can be made to work together for good. Live out this bold and victorious faith in your daily walk.

Let your obstacles be God's opportunities. So you think you can't. Remember: God can. And because God is always able, his words to you, as his faithful follower, are everlastingly these: Sure you can!

Notes

Chapter 1

1. *The Oxford Dictionary of Quotations* (London: Oxford University Press, 1953), p. 293.
2. M. K. W. Heicher, *The Minister's Manual* (New York: Harper & Brothers Publishers, 1959), p. 196.

Chapter 3

1. Howard Norton, excerpt from book, *Rosalynn, a Portrait* (The Atlanta Constitution, October 8, 1977), p. 1A.
2. *Ibid.*
3. *Ibid.*, p. 4A.

Chapter 4

1. *The Atlanta Journal,* Trends of the Times, Editorial Page, October 15, 1952.
2. *Quote Magazine,* quoted from *Successful Farming* (Anderson, S. C., March, 1971), p. 498.
3. Helen Montgomery, *The New Testament in Modern English* (Philadelphia: The Judson Press, 1954).

Chapter 5

1. Piper, Watty, *The Little Engine That Could* (New York: Platt and Munk, 1961).

Chapter 7

1. *The Speaker's Bible*, edited by James Hastings (Grand Rapids: Baker Book House, 1963), Luke, Volume 2, p. 360.
2. *Ibid.*

Chapter 8

1. *Proclaim Magazine* (Nashville: Sunday School Board, July, August, September, 1977), Quoting Hermann Hagedorn, *The Bomb That Fell on America* (New York: Association Press, 1951), pp. 42–43, 52.
2. *Quote Magazine* (Anderson, S. C., September 18, 1977), p. 273.

Chapter 9

1. Piper, Watty, *The Gateway to Storyland* (New York: Platt and Munk, 1969), p. 36.
2. Moffatt, James, *A New Translation of the Bible* (New York: Harper & Brothers, 1950).
3. J. M. Powis Smith and Edgar J. Goodspeed, *The Bible—An American Translation* (Chicago: University of Chicago Press, 1951).
4. J. B. Phillips, *The New Testament in Modern English* (New York: The Macmillan Company, 1959).